D1707965

Career Academies:
Impacts on Students' Initial
Transitions to Post-Secondary
Education and Employment

United States Department of Education
Education Resource Information Center

The BiblioGov Project is an effort to expand awareness of the public documents and records of the U.S. Government via print publications. In broadening the public understanding of government and its work, an enlightened democracy can grow and prosper. Ranging from historic Congressional Bills to the most recent Budget of the United States Government, the BiblioGov Project spans a wealth of government information. These works are now made available through an environmentally friendly, print-on-demand basis, using only what is necessary to meet the required demands of an interested public. We invite you to learn of the records of the U.S. Government, heightening the knowledge and debate that can lead from such publications.

Included are the following Collections:

Budget of The United States Government
Presidential Documents
United States Code
Education Reports from ERIC
GAO Reports
History of Bills
House Rules and Manual
Public and Private Laws

Code of Federal Regulations
Congressional Documents
Economic Indicators
Federal Register
Government Manuals
House Journal
Privacy act Issuances
Statutes at Large

ED 463 412   CE 082 951

AUTHOR   Kemple, James J.
TITLE   Career Academies: Impacts on Students' Initial Transitions
                to Post-Secondary Education and Employment.
INSTITUTION   Manpower Demonstration Research Corp., New York, NY.
SPONS AGENCY   DeWitt Wallace/Reader's Digest Fund, Pleasantville, NY.;
                Ford Foundation, New York, NY.; Department of Education,
                Washington, DC.; Department of Labor, Washington, DC.; Grant
                (W.T.) Foundation, New York, NY.; Pew Charitable Trusts,
                Philadelphia, PA.; Rockefeller Foundation, New York, NY.;
                George Gund Foundation, Cleveland, OH.; Grable Foundation,
                Pittsburgh, PA.; Richard King Mellon Foundation, Pittsburgh,
                PA.; American Express Foundation, New York, NY.; Alcoa
                Foundation, Pittsburgh, PA.; Russell Sage Foundation, New
                York, NY.; Center for Research on the Education of Students
                Placed At Risk, Baltimore, MD.; Westinghouse Foundation,
                Pittsburgh, PA.; Citigroup Foundation, New York, NY.;
                Bristol-Myers Squibb Foundation, Inc., New York, NY.
PUB DATE   2001-12-00
NOTE   75p.; Part of the 10-year Career Academies Evaluation
                project.
AVAILABLE FROM Manpower Demonstration Research Corporation, 16 East 34th
                Street, New York, NY 10016. Tel: 212-532-3200. For full
                text: http://www.mdrc.org/Reports2002/CA_StudentsImpacts/CA_
                StudentImpa ctwTech.pdf.
PUB TYPE   Reports - Evaluative (142)
EDRS PRICE   MF01/PC03 Plus Postage.
DESCRIPTORS   Academic Achievement; Academic Education; *Career Academies;
                *Dropout Prevention; Dropouts; Education Work Relationship;
                Educational Practices; Graduation; High Risk Students; High
                Schools; House Plan; *Integrated Curriculum; Longitudinal
                Studies; *Outcomes of Education; *Program Effectiveness;
                *School Holding Power; Success; Vocational Education

ABSTRACT
        Career academies are characterized by these three basic
features: a school-within-a-school organizational structure, curricula that
combine academic and career or technical courses based on a career theme, and
partnerships with local employers. In a 10-year longitudinal study of the
academy model, begun in 1993 in 9 schools around the country, some 1,700
academy applicants in the 8th or 9th grade were randomly assigned to their
high schools' academy or any other high school program. The evaluation found,
as of the year after scheduled high school graduation, that although the
career academies enhanced the high school experiences of their students in
ways that were consistent with the reform's short-term goals, these positive
effects did not translate into changes in high school graduation rates or
initial transitions to postsecondary education and jobs. Other key findings
included: (1) the academies had little influence on course content, classroom
instructional practices, and standardized test scores; (2) for students at
high risk of dropping out, the academies increased the likelihood of staying
in school through 12th grade, improved attendance, and increased number of
credits earned; and (3) relative to similar students nationally, both studied
groups had high rates of high school graduation, college enrollment, and

Reproductions supplied by EDRS are the best that can be made
from the original document.

employment. The results suggest that career academies should consider expanding their efforts to recruit students who may not be motivated to enroll in academies on their own, to provide college counseling, and to increase teacher professional development activities in order to improve curriculum and instruction. (Contains 25 references, 10 figures, and 6 tables.) (KC)

Reproductions supplied by EDRS are the best that can be made
from the original document.

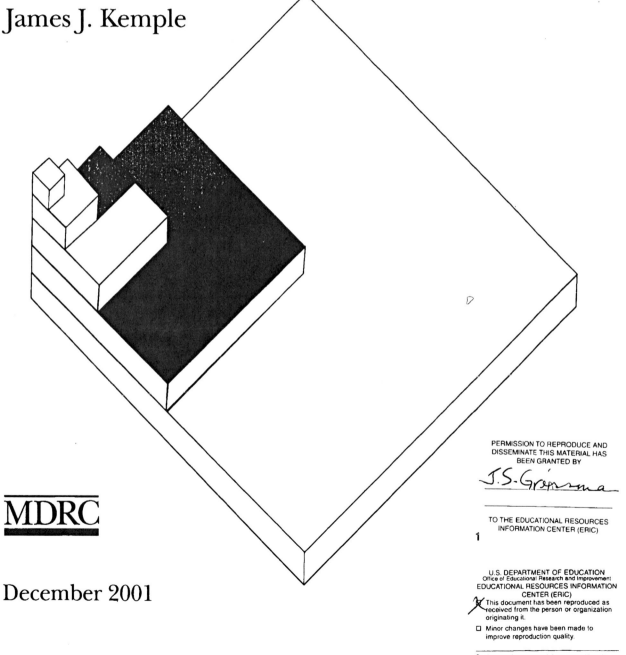

Career Academies

CE

Impacts on Students' Initial Transitions to Post-Secondary Education and Employment

James J. Kemple

MDRC

December 2001

PERMISSION TO REPRODUCE AND
DISSEMINATE THIS MATERIAL HAS
BEEN GRANTED BY

J.S. Gr̃e

TO THE EDUCATIONAL RESOURCES
INFORMATION CENTER (ERIC)

1

U.S. DEPARTMENT OF EDUCATION
Office of Educational Research and Improvement
EDUCATIONAL RESOURCES INFORMATION
CENTER (ERIC)
☒ This document has been reproduced as
received from the person or organization
originating it.
☐ Minor changes have been made to
improve reproduction quality.

° Points of view or opinions stated in this
document do not necessarily represent
official OERI position or policy.

BEST COPY AVAILABLE

2

BOARD OF DIRECTORS

ROBERT SOLOW, *Chairman*
Institute Professor
Massachusetts Institute of Technology

RUDOLPH G. PENNER, *Treasurer*
Senior Fellow
Urban Institute

MARY JO BANE
Professor of Public Policy
John F. Kennedy School of Government
Harvard University

REBECCA M. BLANK
Dean
Gerald R. Ford School of Public Policy
University of Michigan

RON HASKINS
Senior Fellow
Brookings Institution

JAMES H. JOHNSON, JR.
E. Maynard Adams Professor of Business,
    Geography, and Sociology
Director, Urban Investment Strategies Center
University of North Carolina

RICHARD J. MURNANE
Professor of Education
Graduate School of Education
Harvard University

FRANK N. NEWMAN
Chairman Emeritus
Bankers Trust Corporation

JAN NICHOLSON
President
The Grable Foundation

MARION O. SANDLER
Chairman and CEO
Golden West Financial Corporation and
    World Savings and Loan Association

ISABEL V. SAWHILL
Senior Fellow
Brookings Institution

LAWRENCE J. STUPSKI
Chairman
Stupski Family Foundation

WILLIAM JULIUS WILSON
Malcolm Wiener Professor of Social Policy
John F. Kennedy School of Government
Harvard University

JUDITH M. GUERON
President
Manpower Demonstration Research Corporation

BEST COPY AVAILABLE

Career Academies

Impacts on Students' Initial Transitions to Post-Secondary Education and Employment

James J. Kemple

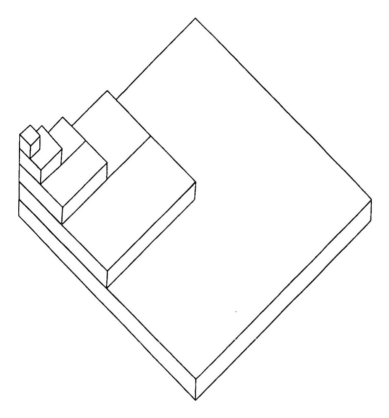

December 2001

Manpower Demonstration Research Corporation

Funders of the Career Academies Evaluation

Wallace–Reader's Digest Funds
Ford Foundation
U.S. Department of Education
U.S. Department of Labor
The Commonwealth Fund
Charles Stewart Mott Foundation
William T. Grant Foundation
The Pew Charitable Trusts
The Rockefeller Foundation
The George Gund Foundation

The Grable Foundation
Richard King Mellon Foundation
American Express Foundation
Alcoa Foundation
Russell Sage Foundation
Center for Research on the Education
   of Students Placed At Risk (CRESPAR)
Westinghouse Foundation
The Citigroup Foundation
Bristol-Myers Squibb Foundation, Inc.

Dissemination of MDRC publications is also supported by the following foundations that help finance MDRC's public policy outreach and expanding efforts to communicate the results and implications of our work to policymakers, practitioners, and others: the Ford, Ewing Marion Kauffman, Ambrose Monell, Alcoa, George Gund, Grable, Anheuser-Busch, New York Times Company, Heinz Family, and Union Carbide Foundations; and the Open Society Institute.

The findings and conclusions in this report do not necessarily represent the official positions or policies of the funders.

For information about MDRC and copies of our publications, see our Web site: www.mdrc.org. MDRC® is a registered trademark of the Manpower Demonstration Research Corporation.

Copyright © 2001 by the Manpower Demonstration Research Corporation. All rights reserved.

Overview

Established more than 30 years ago, Career Academies have spread rapidly over the past decade as states, school districts, and individual schools throughout the country have turned to the approach as part of a solution to a range of problems faced by large comprehensive high schools. Career Academies are typically characterized by three basic features: a school-within-a-school organizational structure, curricula that combine academic and career or technical courses based on a career theme, and partnerships with local employers. The main goals of Academies are to prevent students from dropping out and to prepare them for college and careers.

In 1993, MDRC began conducting the Career Academies Evaluation, a 10-year longitudinal study of the Academy model in nine schools around the country. In the evaluation, more than 1,700 Academy applicants in the 8th or 9th grade were randomly assigned to enroll in their high school's Academy (the Academy group) or to enroll in any other high school program (the non-Academy group). The differences between the two groups' outcomes serve as estimates of the Academies' effects. Owing to its random assignment design, diverse set of participating students and sites, and long follow-up period — which extends four years beyond the students' scheduled graduation from high school — this study is both more comprehensive and more rigorous than previous studies of Academies and other school reforms. The evaluation is being funded by the U.S. Departments of Education and Labor and 17 private foundations and organizations. The new impact findings presented in this report are based on survey data collected about one year after scheduled high school graduation. A later report will present results for the rest of the follow-up period.

Key Findings

Although the participating Career Academies enhanced the high school experiences of their students in ways that are consistent with the reform's short-term goals, these positive effects did not translate into changes in high school graduation rates or initial transitions to post-secondary education and jobs.

- Earlier results from the evaluation indicate that the Academies improved students' high school experiences on several fronts, including their average level of school engagement, the rate at which they combined academic and career-related courses, and the rate at which they participated in career awareness and work-related learning activities. The Academies had little influence, however, on course content and classroom instructional practices and left standardized test scores unchanged.

- For students who entered the programs at high risk of dropping out, the Academies increased the likelihood of staying in school through the end of the 12th-grade year, improved attendance, and increased the number of credits earned toward graduation.

- The results presented in this report show that, relative to similar students nationally, both the Academy and the non-Academy groups had high rates of high school graduation, college enrollment, and employment.

- The Academies had little or no impact on high school graduation rates and initial post-secondary education and employment outcomes. In other words, the Academy group's relatively high outcome levels were matched by those of the non-Academy group — the best benchmark against which to compare the Academy group's performance. This was true for subgroups of students at high, medium, and low dropout risk.

- The results suggest that Career Academies should consider expanding their efforts to recruit students who may not be motivated to enroll in Academies on their own, to provide college counseling from the beginning of high school, and to ensure that teachers have access to professional development opportunities aimed at improving curriculum and instruction.

The new findings go beyond those presented in earlier reports from this evaluation and from previous research on Career Academies. Nevertheless, the full story of Academies' effectiveness is still unfolding. Data collected as the evaluation continues will shed light on any differences between the Academy and non-Academy groups' education and labor market experiences that emerge during the second, third, and fourth years after high school.

Contents

Technical Resources

Amplifying on issues and findings in the report, the Technical Resources are available only on the Web at http://www.mdrc.org/Reports2001/CareerAcademies/CA_TechResources.htm.

     Unit 1: Issues Underlying the Impact Analyses and Comparisons with National Data

     Unit 2: Additional Impacts for the Full Sample

     Unit 3: Additional Impacts for the Risk Subgroups and Impacts for Subgroups
           Defined by Gender, Race, and Educational Expectations

List of Tables and Figures

Preface

The Career Academies Evaluation is aimed at providing reliable evidence about the extent to which Career Academies and related education reforms deliver on an ambitious goal: to transform schools into nurturing environments where all students can acquire the skills needed to succeed in further education and employment. The evaluation is rare among education studies for its design — in which Academy applicants were randomly assigned to a group that enrolled in Academies or to a group that enrolled in other high school programs — and for its long follow-up period, which spanned high school and the years after scheduled graduation.

A milestone in the 10-year project, this report focuses on students' transitions to post-secondary education and jobs during the year after high school. It is being released at a pivotal time for education policymakers and practitioners across the country who are seeking concrete ways to improve high schools and are debating the role of school-to-work programs and career education in this effort. At the federal level, several offices in the U.S. Department of Education are promoting secondary school reform initiatives that include rethinking organizational arrangements, upgrading standards for curriculum and instruction, and building partnerships with employers and other community organizations. In addition, the School-to-Work Opportunities Act recently expired, and Congress will consider reauthorization of the Carl D. Perkins Applied Technology and Vocational Education Act within the next year or two. The goals and organizational components of the Career Academy approach place it at the intersection of these and related reforms.

As the report reveals, the nine Career Academies in the evaluation had little or no impact on students' rates of high school graduation, enrollment in post-secondary education, and employment. Both among Academy and non-Academy students, the outcomes on these measures were comparable to national averages and above average relative to the kind of large urban high schools where the Academy approach is typically implemented. The lack of impacts at this stage may stem partly from the remarkably high performance of the students not enrolled in Academies, all of whom — like the Academy students — took the initiative to apply to an Academy.

Many critics of career and vocational education contend that programs such as Career Academies track students into classes and work experiences that orient them toward immediate entry into the labor market and away from further education. The high outcome levels achieved by the Academy students in this study suggest that these criticisms are not well founded. At the same time, more than a quarter of the Academy students did not graduate on time, and nearly half of them did not enroll in post-secondary education within a year of their scheduled graduation, suggesting that there is room for Academies to improve.

The present findings stand in contrast to those reported earlier from the evaluation. Previous reports found that the Academies positively affected students during high school. But the reports also noted limitations on the Academies' effectiveness that, viewed in the context of the current findings, point to areas where Academy proponents in particular and education policymakers and practitioners more generally may need to devise ways to build on the programs' strengths.

The full story of Career Academies' effectiveness is still unfolding. As the evaluation continues, data on students' education and labor market experiences during the second, third, and fourth years after high school are expected to shed light on whether the Academies enable students to reach higher levels of education and to obtain higher-wage, more career-oriented jobs. We are confident that, in keeping with MDRC's mission, the Career Academies Evaluation will continue to offer policymakers and educators useful lessons about what works for high school students and will demonstrate the value of subjecting promising school reform approaches to rigorous tests of effectiveness.

Robert Ivry
Senior Vice President

Acknowledgments

Like the previous reports from the Career Academies Evaluation, this report is an outgrowth of an extraordinary collaboration between the sites, funders, and advisers who have supported MDRC's efforts over the last eight years. The evaluation would not have been possible without the vision and support of the funding organizations listed at the front of the report. Special gratitude is also due the staff at the participating Career Academies, high schools, school districts, and employer partners as well as the young people who generously gave of their time to respond to the Post-High School Survey. The survey was administered by Anne Van Aman and her associates, who worked tirelessly to find and interview members of the study sample.

The report also benefited greatly from the input of key advisers to the evaluation. Thomas Bailey of Teachers College, Richard Murnane of the Harvard Graduate School of Education, and David Stern of the University of California at Berkeley reviewed an early draft of the findings and provided invaluable advice regarding further analyses and offered insights into the results and their implications.

The following people provided thoughtful feedback on earlier drafts of the report or offered suggestions during briefings at which the findings were presented: Sharon Belli of the U.S. Department of Education's Office of Vocational and Adult Education; Marilyn Binkley of the U.S. Department of Education's Office of Educational Research and Improvement; David Goodwin and Marsha Silverberg of the U.S. Department of Education's Planning and Evaluation Service; Stephanie Powers, former director of the National School-to-Work Office; Ray Uhalde, Marlin Ferral, Gerri Fiala, Lorenzo Harrison, Chris Kulick, Irene Lynn, Eileen Pederson, and Daniel Ryan of the U.S. Department of Labor; Katherine Hughes of the Institute on Education and the Economy; and Tom Smith, consultant to MDRC.

Useful suggestions were also made by the following individuals at the study's private funding organizations in response to drafts of the report or to briefings on the findings: Janice Petrovich and Cyrus Driver of the Ford Foundation, Edward Pauly of the Wallace–Reader's Digest Funds, Terry Savage of the American Express Foundation, Daria Sheehan of the Citigroup Foundation, and Christine Sturgis of the Charles Stewart Mott Foundation.

Leaders from several organizations concerned with Career Academies also provided valuable comments on the findings: Charles Dayton and Susan Tidyman of the Career Academy Support Network, John Ferrandino and Bonnie Silvers of the National Academy Foundation, and Natalie Allen of Philadelphia Academies, Inc., and of the National Career Academy Coalition.

Finally, the following members of MDRC's Education Studies committee offered useful insights on the findings: Richard Murnane, Thomas Bailey, Mary Jo Bane, A. Wade Boykin, Michael Casserly, Jacquelynne Eccles, Eugene Garcia, Richard Elmore, Gerry House, Pedro Noguera, and Charles M. Payne.

From the beginning of the Career Academies Evaluation, Robert Ivry, MDRC's Senior Vice President for Development and External Affairs, has played a pivotal role in building partnerships with the sites, funders, and advisers that form the foundation for the study. This report benefited greatly from his insights and advice on how to sharpen the presentation of the findings and their policy implications. Other MDRC staff members played key roles in acquiring and analyzing data for this report. Marla Sherman coordinated the survey administration and data collection process with Anne Van Aman, and Joel Gordon and Galina Farberova prepared the initial survey data files for analysis.

Judith Scott executed the analyses that produced the findings, provided a wide range of research assistance, prepared the tables and figures, and coordinated the production of this report. Howard Bloom, Fred Doolittle, Judith Gueron, Robert Ivry, Kent McGuire, Marilyn Price, and Jason Snipes reviewed drafts and provided helpful technical and substantive guidance on the presentation. Finally, the author would like to thank Valerie Chase for her insightful comments on the report drafts, thoughtful editing, and efforts to bring the report to publication.

The Author

12

Executive Summary

This report examines how Career Academies, one of the oldest and most widely established high school reforms in the United States, influence students' preparation for and transitions to post-secondary education and the labor market. Since the first Career Academies were established more than 30 years ago, they have been characterized by three features: (1) a school-within-a-school organizational structure aimed at creating a more supportive, personalized learning environment; (2) curricula that combine academic and career or technical courses to enrich teaching and learning; and (3) partnerships with local employers to increase career awareness and provide work-based learning opportunities.

Over the past 10 years, Career Academies have spread rapidly as states, school districts, and individual schools look to the approach as part of a solution to a range of problems facing large comprehensive high schools. The rapid growth of the Academy movement, which now encompasses an estimated 1,500 to 2,500 schools nationwide, has been accompanied by an expansion of the model's target population and goals. Whereas Career Academies originally focused on keeping students at high risk of dropping out enrolled in high school and on readying such students for the world of work, since the early 1990s they have aimed to prepare a mix of high-performing students and high-risk students for both college and employment. These developments have fueled the need for reliable evidence about how Career Academies affect students' performance in high school and their transitions to further education and careers.

With funding from the U.S. Departments of Education and Labor and 17 private foundations and organizations, the Manpower Demonstration Research Corporation (MDRC) began evaluating the Career Academy approach in 1993. The Career Academies Evaluation is one of the few studies of a school reform initiative that compares the experiences of students who applied to participate in the initiative and were randomly selected to enroll (the Academy group) with those of students in the same schools who applied for the initiative but were randomly selected not to enroll (the non-Academy group). The differences between the two groups serve as estimates of the Academies' impacts on students' outcomes. This type of research design is widely considered to be the most reliable way to measure the effectiveness of selective, voluntary interventions such as Career Academies. The evaluation is also unusual among studies of school reforms for following both groups of students from the beginning of high school through several years after graduation.

The nine participating high schools had implemented the three basic features of the Career Academy approach when they were selected for inclusion in the evaluation. As a group, they reflect the typical conditions under which Academies have operated during the past decade: All are located in or near urban areas, and each school's Academy sought to serve a mix of students ranging from those at high risk of dropping out to those highly engaged in school.

Focusing on the year after students' scheduled graduation from high school, this report examines these Career Academies' effects on graduation rates, post-secondary education enrollment, and labor market participation. The primary data were obtained from a survey administered to nearly 1,500 students in the study sample — about half of whom had been randomly assigned to Academies and about half of whom had been randomly assigned to other high school programs — approximately 14 months after their scheduled high school graduation (hereafter referred to as the "year after scheduled graduation" or the "year after high school").

Previously Reported Findings

Evidence presented in previous reports from the evaluation indicates that the participating Career Academies changed students' high school experiences in ways that are consistent with the short-term goals of the Academy approach:

- Relative to other high school programs, the Academies increased the level of interpersonal support that students received from their teachers and peers.

- Compared with their non-Academy counterparts, Academy students were more likely to combine academic and career or technical courses and to participate in career awareness and work-based learning activities.

- For students who entered the programs at high risk of dropping out, the Academies increased the likelihood of staying in school through the end of the 12th-grade year, the attendance rate, and the number of credits earned toward graduation.

- For students at medium or low risk of dropping out, the Academies increased access to career or technical courses and raised participation in career development activities without reducing academic course-taking.

Previously reported findings also revealed the following limits on the Academies' effectiveness:

- More than one-third of the students who enrolled in the Academies left the programs before the end of their 12th-grade year.

- The Academies that did not increase the interpersonal supports that students received from teachers and peers reduced student engagement — as reflected in school attendance, course-taking, and dropout rates — for some students.

- The Academies had little influence on course content and instructional practices and did not affect standardized test scores for any subgroup of students.

New Findings

The evidence presented in this report addresses three key questions:

1. What were the high school graduation rates and early college and work experiences of the non-Academy students, who in this research design set the standard against which Academy students are compared?

2. What impacts did the Career Academies have on these outcomes?

3. To what extent did the Career Academies' impacts differ across subgroups of students with characteristics associated with being at high, medium, or low risk of dropping out of high school?

Following is a summary of the findings.

- Relative to similar students nationally, the non-Academy group achieved high rates of high school graduation, college enrollment, and employment.

Owing to the study's random assignment research design — which ensures that there were no systematic differences between the Academy and non-Academy groups at the outset of the study — the outcomes for the non-Academy group are the best benchmark against which to measure the impacts of the Career Academies on the Academy group. As shown in Table ES.1, which presents several key outcomes for the non-Academy group, a large majority of non-Academy students graduated from high school on time, and a majority went on to post-secondary education programs during the following year.

Table ES.1 places the non-Academy outcomes in the context of outcomes for a nationally representative group of students with similar background characteristics who were enrolled in urban comprehensive public schools. The non-Academy students generally fared better than similar students who were enrolled in career or technical programs, on a par with or better than students in general curriculum programs, and somewhat worse than students enrolled in academic or college preparatory programs. Overall, the performance of the non-Academy group thus sets a formidable standard for the Academy group to exceed.

- On average, the Career Academies had little impact on high school graduation rates and initial post-secondary outcomes. The relatively high outcome levels achieved by Academy students were matched by those for their non-Academy counterparts.

Table ES.2, which presents the high school completion, post-secondary education enrollment, and employment rates for the Academy and non-Academy groups, makes clear that there were virtually no differences between the groups during the year after scheduled high school graduation. The lack of impacts on these transitional outcomes appears to be inconsistent with the substantial differences between Academy and non-Academy students' high school experiences documented in previous reports from the study. Two factors may help account for the discrepancies. First, judging from the non-Academy group's high outcomes relative to those for national samples, it appears that the students who applied to the Career Academies would have found other routes to graduation and post-secondary education without the programs. Second, the benefits that accrued to Academy students during high school may not have related directly enough to students' immediate post-high school transitions or may not have been substantial enough to affect these transitions. Longer-term follow-up will reveal whether the benefits eventually lead to higher levels of educational attainment or greater labor market success.

- Among students at high risk of dropping out, the Career Academies' impacts were less pronounced during the year after high school than they were during high school.

Table ES.1

Outcomes for the Non-Academy Group and the NELS Sample

Outcome (%)	Non-Academy Group	NELS Sample		
		Career/ Technical	General	Academic
Earned high school diploma or GED	86.7	81.4	86.2	88.5
On-time graduate	74.4	63.8	68.8	84.7
Late graduate	7.4	14.0	11.3	3.5
Earned a GED or other certificate	5.0	3.6	6.1	0.3
Enrolled in post-secondary education degree program	54.6	41.8	43.9	53.5
Bachelor's degree program	15.5	20.7	15.6	26.1
Associate's degree program	27.8	17.0	17.5	18.6
Skills training program	11.3	4.1	10.8	8.8
Ever employed	87.2	84.5	82.6	80.0
Sample size	665	269	886	744

SOURCE: MDRC calculations from the Career Academies Evaluation Post-High School Follow-Up Survey Database and the National Education Longitudinal Study (NELS), 1988-1994 data.

NOTES: All measures reflect status at the end of August in the year following scheduled high school graduation.

The NELS sample includes only students who were enrolled in a nonselective urban public high school in 10th grade.

Students were considered on-time graduates if they received their diploma by the end of June in the year they were scheduled to graduate.

Post-secondary education measures reflect the highest degree programs in which students enrolled. Students must have earned a high school diploma or GED to be considered enrolled in these programs.

Ever employed means having ever worked for pay during the follow-up period.

MDRC estimates were regression-adjusted using ordinary least squares, controlling for background characteristics.

The NELS estimates were regression-adjusted and mean-centered to reflect outcomes for students who had the same distribution of background characteristics as non-Academy sample members.

No tests of statistical significance were performed.

Table ES.2

Impacts on High School Completion, Post-Secondary Education, and Employment

Outcome (%)	Academy Group	Non-Academy Group	Impact (Difference)	Percentage Change
Earned high school diploma or GED	87.2	86.7	0.5	0.6
On-time graduate	74.0	74.4	-0.4	-0.5
Late graduate	5.8	7.4	-1.6	-21.8
Earned a GED or other certificate	7.5	5.0	2.5	49.6
Enrolled in post-secondary education degree program	54.8	54.6	0.2	0.3
Bachelor's degree program	14.7	15.5	-0.9	-5.6
Associate's degree program	27.3	27.8	-0.5	-1.8
Skills training program	12.8	11.3	1.6	13.9
Ever employed	88.7	87.2	1.5	1.7
Sample size (N=1,482)	817	665		

SOURCE: MDRC calculations from the Career Academies Evaluation Post-High School Follow-Up Survey Database.

NOTES: All measures reflect status at the end of August in the year following scheduled high school graduation.

Students were considered on-time graduates if they received their diploma by the end of June in the year they were scheduled to graduate.

The post-secondary education measures reflect the highest degree programs in which students enrolled. Students must have earned a high school diploma or GED to be considered enrolled in these programs.

Percentage change equals the impact divided by the non-Academy group average.

Ever employed means having ever worked for pay during the follow-up period.

Estimates were regression-adjusted using ordinary least squares, controlling for background characteristics.

A two-tailed t-test was applied to differences between the Academy and non-Academy groups. The difference in receipt of a GED or other certificate was statistically significant at the 5 percent level. No other differences between the Academy and non-Academy groups in this table were statistically significant.

Earlier findings from the evaluation indicate that the Academies increased school engagement — as reflected in higher school attendance rates and lower dropout rates — and facilitated progress toward graduation among students who entered the programs at high risk of dropping out. The findings in the current report are more mixed. For the high-risk subgroup, the Academies led to a modest (though not statistically significant) increase in the on-time graduation rate and in the likelihood of completing a basic academic core curriculum. Also, the Academies produced a statistically significant increase in the proportion of high-risk students who earned a one-year post-secondary license or certificate. During the year after scheduled graduation, however, students in the non-Academy group "caught up" with Academy students by graduating from high school late and enrolling in bachelor's or associate's degree programs at about the same rates as the Academy students. By the end of the year after high school, there was virtually no difference between the Academy and non-Academy students in the high-risk subgroup in the amount of time spent attending post-secondary education, working, or combining the two.

- In general, the findings for students who entered the program at medium or low risk of dropping out of high school were consistent with those for the full sample: Academy and non-Academy students did well relative to national samples, but the two groups' education and labor market outcomes were comparable.

With few exceptions, the Academies had no impacts on key transitional outcomes for students in the medium- and low-risk subgroups. For the medium-risk subgroup, there were two notable statistically significant impacts. On the one hand, the Academy group was somewhat more likely to earn a General Educational Development (GED) credential instead of a high school diploma. On the other hand, although the Academy and non-Academy students in the medium-risk subgroup were equally likely to be employed during the year after high school, the jobs held by Academy group members paid a higher average hourly wage.

Implications

- The findings indicate that Career Academies offer a viable pathway to high school graduation and post-secondary education.

Career Academies have been associated most notably with career and technical education and the school-to-work movement. Some critics of Career Academies and related education strategies have argued that Academies primarily target students who do not plan to go to college, tracking them into classes and work experiences that orient them toward immediate entry into the labor market. Other critics maintain that Career Academies induce college-bound students who are attracted to the programs to substitute career and technical classes and work experience for academic classes and experiences that would qualify them for college.

Overall, the present findings suggest that neither line of criticism is well founded. The Career Academies in this evaluation prepared most of their students to graduate from high school and enroll in post-secondary education. In fact, Academy students reached these milestones at rates roughly comparable to those for similar students in urban public schools across the country. Some researchers and policymakers have suggested that large comprehensive high schools such as those in this study do not offer enough pathways from high school to post-secondary education to accommodate all students. The Career Academy approach may afford one way to expand the set of available pathways, at least for students who have the initiative to apply for them.

> o Academies changed the high school environments and experiences of their students and teachers in ways that were consistent with the program's short-term goals. Yet these changes did not translate into different initial post-secondary education experiences than would have been expected for equally motivated students not enrolled in Academies.

Evidence from this evaluation and others indicates that Career Academies improve students' high school experiences. While the small learning communities probably account for the stronger interpersonal supports and higher levels of engagement among Academy students, the career themes provide a framework for combining academic and career-related courses, and the employer partnerships afford students greater access to career development experiences and work-based learning opportunities.

Beyond these short-term outcomes, however, the Academies' impacts appear to dissipate. As discussed in a previous report from this study, the participating Career Academies — though they created conditions for maintaining and even enhancing students' engagement in high school — did not change classroom instruction substantially or affect standardized measures of academic achievement. Similarly, most of the participating Academies did not provide college counseling services tailored for Academy students or to their needs and interests, which may help explain the lack of impacts on post-secondary education enrollments.

> o The present findings challenge Career Academy proponents and education policymakers to build on the strengths of the approach as they attempt to raise rates of high school completion and enrollment in post-secondary education.

More than 25 percent of the students in the Academy group did not graduate from high school on time; approximately 45 percent had not enrolled in a post-secondary education program by the end of the year after scheduled graduation; and only 15 percent enrolled in bachelor's degree programs. These findings suggest that, although the Academy students did as well or better than national samples of similar students in similar programs, there is room for improvement. At this point in the evaluation, it is possible only to suggest some hypotheses about how the Career Academy approach might effect these improvements.

Increase high-risk students' access to Career Academies. To the extent that Academies have longer-term impacts, the impacts are concentrated among students who entered the program at high risk of dropping out. This finding suggests that Academies should make greater efforts to attract and retain such students. At the same time, targeting the programs exclusively to high-risk students might lower teachers', students', and parents' expectations of the program. More importantly, based on implementation research conducted for this evaluation, the Academies appear to draw at least some of their power to improve interpersonal supports and to increase student engagement from the diversity of their student bodies.

Heighten the emphasis on meeting academic standards, and provide more intensive guidance and support for college entrance. The Academy model has been shown to address such problems as low student engagement, learning activities that have little relevance to students, and weak connections between schools on the one hand and local communities and the world of work on the other. The approach appears to be less well equipped to improve other outcomes, such as standardized test scores and rates of enrollment in four-year colleges. Academy proponents and policymakers should develop strategies for addressing these limitations directly. For example, school officials and Academy administrators might consider implementing an accelerated academic program in the 9th grade to help students who are behind academically to catch up. In grades 10 to 12, the Academies could then focus on providing students with a rigorous academic curriculum of higher-level courses that would prepare them for high-stakes tests and help them garner the credentials needed to attend college. It is also critical to provide college and career counseling throughout high school and to monitor students' progress both in and outside the classroom.

Next Steps in the Evaluation

Although the results presented in this report go beyond those presented in other research on Career Academies and in previous reports from this evaluation, the full story of Career Academies' effectiveness is still unfolding. Indeed, the findings reported to date point to the need to examine longer-term results before making definitive judgments about the effectiveness of the approach.

Earlier results from the Career Academies Evaluation show that the Academies expanded students' exposure to career awareness and development activities and work-related learning opportunities. Moreover, consistent with studies indicating that the year after high school graduation is a particularly unsettled period for 18- to 20-year-old youth, the Academy and non-Academy students in this study exhibited a relatively high rate of enrollment in one- and two-year post-secondary degree programs, and many made multiple transitions between education and employment opportunities. Finally, a more definitive assessment of the strengths and limitations of the Career Academy approach — a school-to-career initiative — should include evidence about its longer-term effects on educational attainment and employment outcomes.

To address these and other issues, the evaluation is collecting data on students' education and labor market experiences during the second, third, and fourth years after scheduled high school graduation. The goal of this ongoing work is to determine whether the Academies enable students to make better choices about post-secondary education and employment and, if so, whether their choices lead to higher educational attainment and entry into higher-wage, more career-oriented jobs.

Report

I. Introduction

This report examines how Career Academies, one of the oldest and most widely established high school reforms in the United States, influence students' preparation for and transitions to post-secondary education and the labor market. Since the first Career Academies were established more than 30 years ago, they have had three distinguishing features: (1) they are organized as a school-within-a-school to create a more supportive, personalized learning environment; (2) they combine academic and career and technical curricula around a career theme to enrich teaching and learning; and (3) they establish partnerships with local employers to provide career awareness and work-based learning opportunities for students. Although the basic organizational features of the approach have remained the same since its inception, its goals and target population have changed. The original Academies were designed primarily to keep students at risk of dropping out enrolled in high school and to increase such students' preparedness for work. There is now widespread agreement that Career Academies should serve a broad population, including students who are highly engaged in school and students who are at risk of dropping out, and should seek to prepare students for both college and work.

Over the past decade, Career Academies have proliferated more rapidly than ever. National, state, and local networks of Academies have grown significantly, while the Career Academy model has been incorporated, in whole or in part, into other school reform initiatives. Academies now stand at the intersection of several high school reform movements, including efforts to build school-to-work systems, to reconstitute vocational and technical education, to effect comprehensive school change, and to break large high schools into smaller learning communities. Many of these initiatives are tied to federal and state legislation that point to the Career Academy approach as reflecting their policy goals. In addition, local school districts and individual high schools have looked to the Career Academy model as a concrete approach to realizing these and other policy initiatives.

The expansion of the Career Academy approach, the extension of its target population and goals, and the growth of related reforms have fueled the need for reliable evidence about Academies' effects. In 1993, the Manpower Demonstration Research Corporation (MDRC) began a uniquely rigorous evaluation of the Career Academy approach in a diverse set of nine high schools across the country. The evaluation's primary goal is to provide policymakers and educators with reliable evidence about how Career Academies affect students' performance and engagement during high school and their later transitions to post-secondary education and the labor market. It also aims to provide information about how the programs operate and to examine factors that may enhance or undermine their effectiveness. The evaluation is funded by the U.S. Departments of Education and Labor and by 17 private foundations and organizations.

This report, the fifth from the evaluation, examines the participating Career Academies' effects on high school graduation rates and on the rates at which students in the study enrolled in post-secondary education programs during the year after scheduled high school graduation. It also includes information about the rates at which students worked and combined school and work. A later report will examine the Academies' effects on educational attainment, labor market participation, and life experiences over four years after high school.

The next section describes the Career Academy approach in detail, highlights the key features of this evaluation, and briefly summarizes the findings from previous reports. The third section describes the types of data used to capture students' initial post-high school experiences and examines several analytical issues critical to interpreting the findings discussed in the remainder of the report. To provide a context for the findings, the high school completion and post-secondary education statuses of students in the Career Academies Evaluation are then compared with those of a national sample of students with similar characteristics. The remainder of the report presents the program's effects on the full study sample and on subgroups of students defined by characteristics associated with being at risk of dropping out of high school. The final section discusses some implications that the study findings may have for education policy and practice.[1]

II.   Career Academies: The Approach and This Evaluation

A. The Career Academy Approach

The durability and broad appeal of the Career Academy approach are partly attributable to the fact that its core features offer direct responses to a number of problems common in large comprehensive high schools, particularly in urban schools that serve low-income students. The following constitute the basic elements of a Career Academy. First, a Career Academy is organized as a *school-within-a-school* — or a "small learning community" — in which students stay with the same group of teachers over three or four years during high school. The aim is to create a more personalized, supportive learning environment for students and teachers. Second, a Career Academy offers students a combination of *academic and career-related curricula* and uses a career theme to integrate the two. Third, a Career Academy establishes *partnerships with local employers* in an effort to build connections between school and work and to provide students with a range of career development and work-based learning opportunities. This definition of an Academy, now commonly accepted, was reviewed by a broad range of researchers, policymakers, and practitioners who have worked closely with Career Academies.[2]

The early Career Academies, which operated in the 1970s and 1980s, were primarily vocational education programs targeted at students who appeared to be at high risk of dropping out of high school. The central goals of those programs were to keep students engaged in school, provide them with work-related learning experiences both in the classroom and on the job, and establish clearer pathways between high school and post-secondary employment.

Since the late 1980s, the primary goals and target population of most Career Academies have shifted. In particular, there is now wide agreement that the Career Academy approach

---

[1]For the Technical Resources for this report — which include information about the samples, measures, and analytical methods used to derive the findings and supplementary tables presenting detailed findings for the full study sample and various subgroups — see Kemple (2001).

[2]Career Academy Support Network, 2001.

should distinguish itself from traditional vocational education by seeking to prepare students for both work and college. Vocational education, as defined in federal law and by historical precedent, has been directed at preparing young people for occupations that do not traditionally require advanced degrees. In line with what has been called "the new vocational education," Career Academies now seek to include a wide cross section of students and to combine a rigorous academic curriculum with exposure to extensive information about an industry both in the workplace and in the classroom. The career theme used to integrate curricula is intended to provide exposure to a broad array of careers in a given field rather than to prepare students for specific jobs in that field.

Figure 1 illustrates a conceptual model of the pathways through which the Career Academy approach is hypothesized to affect students' outcomes during high school and thereafter. The figure lists the three basic organizational elements of the Career Academy approach in the first column and shows how they are hypothesized to give rise to the three types of supports and learning opportunities in the second column: (1) The intensive collaboration afforded by the school-within-a-school organization is hypothesized to enhance interpersonal supports; (2) the combination of academic and vocational courses is hypothesized to help focus curricula and enrich teaching and learning; and (3) the employer partnerships are hypothesized to increase career awareness and work-based learning opportunities. Together the supports and learning opportunities are intended to increase students' engagement in school (as reflected, for example, in school attendance), prevent them from dropping out, enhance their academic performance, encourage them to use their nonschool hours constructively and to avoid risk-taking behaviors (such as criminal activity and drug use), and help them meet graduation requirements. The ultimate goal of Career Academies is to prepare young people for postsecondary education and employment.

During the mid and late 1990s, education policymakers and practitioners began pursuing a number of far-reaching strategies for improving high schools in the United States. Some of these efforts fell under the umbrella of the school-to-work movement, whereas others came under the rubric of "comprehensive" school reforms (the latter aim to reform entire schools through changes in governance, curriculum, and organization). Many of these strategies include principles embedded in the Career Academy approach, while others include the Career Academy model as an explicit component. There are now estimated to be between 1,500 and 2,500 Career Academies nationwide, more than 10 times as many as during the late 1980s.[3] Much of this growth can be traced to the increasing number of national, state, and district Academy support networks. Although most Career Academies share the approach's basic elements, the Academy model has been adapted to a wide range of local needs and circumstances.

---

[3]Stern, Dayton, and Raby, 2000.

23

Career Academies Evaluation

Figure 1

Conceptual Model
of the Career Academy Approach

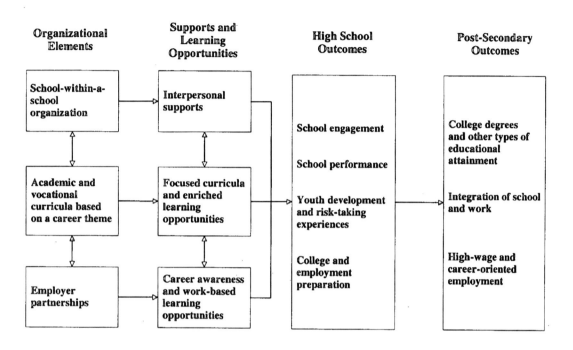

-4-

24

B. The Career Academies Evaluation

Over the past 15 years, researchers have conducted numerous studies of Career Academies.[4] Several studies documented the feasibility and institutional growth of the Career Academy approach in a single school, school district, or state. Other studies assessed Academies' effects on students' high school performance and graduation rates, enrollment in post-secondary education, and labor market participation. In general, past research on the effects of Career Academies suggests that Academy students have better attendance, grades, and graduation rates than other students with similar background characteristics. The few studies that attempted to follow students after high school found evidence suggesting that Academy students are more likely to enroll in post-secondary education programs than other students with similar background characteristics.[5] Both lines of research are sometimes taken to indicate that Career Academies are responsible for Academy students' better outcomes.

Recent trends in the Career Academy movement in particular and in the policy environment more generally have increased the demand for more reliable, extensive evidence about the effectiveness of the approach. As already noted, there are now an unprecedented number of Academies nationwide, and the Academies in this new generation have broader goals and aim to serve a wider spectrum of students than did their precursors. Academies are also being promoted as a response to federal policy initiatives including the School-to-Work Opportunities Act of 1994, the Comprehensive School Reform Demonstration, the Carl D. Perkins Vocational and Applied Technology Act of 1998, and the Smaller Learning Communities Program. These trends raise questions like the following: How well does the Academy approach meet the needs of a much wider spectrum of students than it was initially designed to serve? To what extent is it more effective under some conditions than under others? Which features of the Academy model make the most difference for students? How well do Career Academies meet the needs of federal, state, and local policy initiatives?

The Career Academies Evaluation, which was designed to address these questions, offers at least four advantages over previous research on Career Academies:

1. a random assignment research design — the most rigorous way to measure a program's effects;

2. a longitudinal database that will eventually include four years of post-high school follow-up data to learn about Academy and non-Academy students' educational attainment and labor market experiences;

3. a diverse group of sites (schools and districts) that reflect the typical conditions under which the Career Academy approach has been implemented and sustained;

4. a focus on the effectiveness of Academies across their new broader target population of students and new wider spectrum of goals.

---

[4]For a recent summary of this research, see Stern, Dayton, and Raby (2000).
[5]See Maxwell and Rubin, 1997, 1999, 2000.

Following is a description of these key features of the evaluation.

A random assignment research design. The research designs used in previous studies have left uncertainties about the reliability of the findings of program effects. Researchers working on these studies have recognized that their findings may overestimate, or even underestimate, the true effects of Academies on student outcomes.[6] Most importantly, there have been uncertainties about whether the relatively high performance levels of Career Academy students are actually attributable to the services provided by Academies.

On the one hand, because Academies are typically voluntary programs, good student performance results at least partly from the extra motivation or other characteristics of the students who were attracted to Academies rather than from their experiences in the programs. In other words, Academies may attract students (even among those whose background characteristics indicate a risk of dropping out) who would have been motivated enough to do well even if they had not been in the program. Thus, comparing these students with students who are not motivated to apply for an Academy may result in overestimates of the program's true effects. On the other hand, many Academies expressly aim to serve at-risk students. In studies where such students are compared with the general high school population, which probably includes a higher proportion of high-performing students, the true effects of the programs may actually be underestimated. Many researchers in past evaluations of Career Academies have emphasized that a random assignment research design would be necessary to rule out such systematic overestimates and underestimates of Academies' effects.

The Career Academies Evaluation is rare in the field of education research in that it has demonstrated the feasibility and benefits of implementing a large-scale, multisite random assignment research design within an ongoing high school program. There is wide agreement that this is the most reliable approach to measuring the effects of programs like Career Academies.[7] The random assignment design used in this evaluation was made possible by the fact that each of the nine Career Academies in the study had more than twice as many applicants as it was able to serve. Knowing that the program would therefore have to be "rationed" in their schools, the participating Academies worked with MDRC to implement a random process for selecting eligible applicants to fill their Academies rather than selecting on some other basis.[8]

The research sample for the evaluation includes 1,764 students who applied to enroll in a Career Academy. Approximately 55 percent of these applicants, the *Academy group,* were randomly selected to enroll in the Academies. The remaining 45 percent of students, the *non-Academy group*, were not invited to enroll. The non-Academy students either continued to attend the general high school program in which they were enrolled or selected options other than the Academy that were on offer in the same high school or in the same school district. The differences between the two groups' outcomes serve as estimates of the Academies' *impacts* on stu-

---

[6]See, for example, Stern, Dayton, and Raby, 2000; and Maxwell and Rubin, 2000.

[7]See Betsey, Hollister, and Papageorgiou, 1985; Job Training Partnership Act, 1989; Atkinson and Jackson, 1992.

[8]For a detailed description of how the random assignment procedures were implemented for this evaluation, see Kemple and Rock (1996).

dents' outcomes. As discussed below, data are being collected for the sample members in both groups over an eight-year period starting at their high school entry.

The random assignment process ensured that, at the outset of the study, there were no systematic differences between the two groups of students in terms of their background characteristics, prior school experiences, or initial motivation and attitudes toward school. Any systematic differences that subsequently emerge between the groups can therefore be attributed with confidence to differences in their access and exposure to the Career Academies.

A longitudinal database. Resource limitations and other constraints on data collection prevented previous studies from compiling information that could be used to determine the long-term effects of Career Academies on a wide spectrum of educational and labor market outcomes. To overcome these obstacles, this evaluation built a consortium of public and private funders and established an extensive longitudinal data collection system.

Each student in the evaluation sample applied to an Academy and was randomly assigned to one of the research groups at the end of the 8th or 9th grade. Data have been collected from a variety of sources including school transcript records; surveys that students completed at various points during high school; standardized math computation and reading comprehension tests administered to a subsample of students at the end of their scheduled 12th-grade year; and qualitative field research conducted throughout the evaluation to document the participating Academies' implementation, local contexts, staff, students, and employer partners.

Previous reports from the evaluation followed students in both the Academy and non-Academy groups through the end of their scheduled 12th-grade year, that is, until just before they would have graduated from high school. The new data presented in this report were obtained from a survey that students completed somewhat more than a year after their scheduled graduation.

A diverse group of participating sites. A third important set of questions that has not received much attention in previous research concerns the variation in Career Academies' effectiveness across a wide range of contexts and networks. This evaluation focuses on nine high schools that were strategically selected for, among other characteristics, serving a diverse group of students.[9] As a group the sites reflect the typical conditions under which Career Academies have been implemented across the country, and as individuals they capture much of the variation in the approach as it has been tailored to local needs and circumstances.

Each of the high schools in the study is located in or near a large urban school district that serves a substantially higher percentage of African-American and Hispanic students than school districts nationally. On average, the school districts in which these Academies are located also have higher dropout rates, higher unemployment rates, and higher percentages of low-income families than do school districts nationally. Consistent with the Academy model's new, broader

---

[9]For a more detailed description of the criteria and process used to select sites for this study, see Kemple and Rock (1996). Ten sites were initially selected, but one of the Academies was disbanded two years into the study period and was therefore unable to provide sufficient follow-up data to be included in subsequent analysis of students' experiences and outcomes.

scope, each Academy sought to serve a mix of students, including students with characteristics associated with dropping out of high school and students who entered high school highly engaged in school and performing well academically.

Each of the Academies had implemented the basic Career Academy components described earlier: a school-within-a-school organization, a curriculum that integrated academic and vocational coursework, and employer partnerships. This combination of features was not available through other programs in the participating high schools. Although some of the participating schools operated other programs that they classified as "academies," information collected for this study indicated that such programs did not include all the basic components of the Academy approach described above. As a result, the participating Career Academies represent a clear contrast with the other programs in the host high schools.

In summary, the sites participating in the Career Academies Evaluation provide a foundation on which to build a credible assessment of the implementation and impacts of the Career Academy approach. Three important caveats should be kept in mind, however, in interpreting the findings from this study — particularly those in this report.

First, because the participating sites were chosen strategically rather than randomly, the findings from this study cannot necessarily be generalized to all schools and school districts. Nevertheless, as a group these sites typify urban schools and school districts of moderate size, reflecting much of the diversity of such places.

Second, like their host high schools and school districts, the participating Career Academies are dynamic and evolving. Over the study period, most of the programs have modified various components of the Career Academy approach in response to changing conditions in their host high schools or school districts, and many of them have moved toward realizing more complete versions of the model. Others were weakened by staff turnover, decreases in funding, changes in local or state education policy, fluctuating levels of support from building or district staff, and changes in the amount and types of support provided by employer partners.

Third, each Academy in this evaluation operated as a single, relatively independent school-within-a-school, or a "pocket Academy." Throughout the 30-year history of Career Academies, this has been the typical organizational arrangement. More recently, a few school districts have begun to convert entire high schools into clusters of Career Academies, or a "wall-to-wall Academy." In such schools, all students must choose an Academy or Academy-like program. As a result, caution should be exercised when attempting to apply the findings from this evaluation to wall-to-wall Academies, which represent a dramatic departure from the approach taken in the pocket Academies examined here.

A diverse group of students. The student populations in Career Academies tend to reflect the ethnic, gender, and socioeconomic characteristics of their host high schools, which are increasingly diverse. Moreover, with their expanded goals, Academies now attract students with a wider range of needs and interests than they did in the past. Little is known about the relative effectiveness of Academies for key subgroups. For instance, some students who apply for Academies at the end of the 8th or 9th grade are already highly engaged in school. A key goal of Academies is to prepare such students for college and to provide them with career-related learning ex-

28

periences and credentials that will make them more competitive in the labor market. At the other extreme, some Academy applicants are already on a path toward dropping out or having their education end with high school. Academies need to help "reengage" these students, providing them with more applied learning experiences and encouraging them to develop higher aspirations for both education and employment. More needs to be learned about the suitability of the Academy approach for meeting the needs of students in different groups.

To assess the variation in program impacts across this diverse group of students, the Career Academies Evaluation has estimated impacts on subgroups of students defined by background characteristics and prior school experiences associated with dropping out of high school. Following are brief definitions of the three *risk subgroups* that have been the focus of the findings in previous reports and are examined here as well. Each of the characteristics used to define these subgroups was measured at the time that students applied for a Career Academy, that is, before they were randomly selected to be in the Academy or the non-Academy group.[10]

1. **High-risk subgroup**: students in the study sample (approximately 25 percent of both the Academy and the non-Academy groups) with the combination of characteristics associated with the highest likelihood of dropping out

2. **Medium-risk subgroup**: students in the study sample (approximately 50 percent of both the Academy and the non-Academy groups) who had characteristics indicating that they were not particularly likely to drop out but were not highly engaged in school.

3. **Low-risk subgroup**: students in the study sample (approximately 25 percent of both the Academy and the non-Academy groups) with the combination of characteristics associated with the lowest likelihood of dropping out

C. Summary of Previous Findings from the Evaluation

The first three previous reports from the evaluation described the implementation of the core elements of the Career Academy approach and assessed the extent to which these elements provided students, teachers, and employers with the types of supports and learning opportunities outlined in Figure 1.[11] The fourth report examined the impact that the participating Academies had on students' performance and engagement through the end of their 12th-grade year in high

---

[10]The definition of these subgroups is based on analyses using background characteristics to predict dropping out among students in the non-Academy group. These analyses yielded an index that expressed dropout risk as the weighted average of selected background characteristics. The index was then calculated for the Academy group using the same characteristics. Because the predicted relationship between background characteristics and dropout rates was based on information about the non-Academy group, however, it is likely to yield somewhat more accurate predictions of likely dropouts for that group than for the Academy group. Therefore, the dropout rate actually observed for the students in the high-risk non-Academy group may be artificially high. Extensive analyses were conducted to identify the magnitude of this potential distortion. These analyses indicate that whatever distortion exists is minimal and could not have changed the patterns of impacts presented in any of the reports from the evaluation. For a detailed discussion of the method used to define the risk subgroups, see Kemple and Snipes (2000).

[11]See Kemple and Rock, 1996; Kemple, 1997; and Kemple, Poglinco, and Snipes, 1999.

school.[12] Following is a brief overview of the key findings and conclusions presented in those reports.

Several findings indicate that the participating Career Academies changed students' experiences during high school in ways that are highly consistent with the short-term goals of the Academy approach:

o Relative to other high school programs, the Academies increased the level of interpersonal supports that students received from their teachers and peers.

o Compared with their non-Academy counterparts, Academy students were more likely to combine academic and career or technical courses and to participate in career awareness and work-based learning activities.

o For students who entered the programs at high risk of dropping out, the Academies increased the likelihood of staying in school through the end of the 12th-grade year, improved attendance, and increased the number of credits earned toward graduation.

o For students at medium or low risk of dropping out, the Academies increased career and technical course-taking and participation in career development activities without reducing academic course-taking.

Previously reported findings also indicate several limitations on the Academies' effectiveness:

o One-third of the students who initially enrolled in the Academies left the programs before the end of their 12th-grade year.

o The Academies that did not substantially increase interpersonal supports from teachers and peers reduced engagement and academic course-taking for some students.

o The curriculum and instructional strategies used in Academy courses were generally similar to those used in courses offered in the rest of the high school.

o The Academies had no impact on standardized test scores for the full sample or for any of the risk subgroups.

Not surprisingly, the Academies appear to have been most effective at influencing those aspects of school functioning and student and teacher experiences that are closest to the core features of the approach. For example, the Academies' school-within-a-school organization appeared to create communities of support for teachers and students. In this context, students were more highly engaged in school, which was reflected in high attendance rates, low dropout rates, and — in the words of several students — a sense of being in a "family-like" atmosphere. Teachers too saw the Academies as a "learning community" in which they collaborated with colleagues and were able to give students more personalized attention. The findings suggest that these types

---

[12]See Kemple and Snipes, 2000.

of interpersonal supports may have paved the way for the positive effects that the Academies had on student engagement. The Academies that did not increase interpersonal supports (relative to what was already available in the regular high school environment) were more likely to have students become disengaged and even drop out of high school.

Another key feature of the Career Academy approach — employer partnerships — offered employers structured, concrete opportunities to engage in the educational mission of high schools. These partnerships provided students with a broad array of career awareness and development experiences both in and outside school, including work-based learning internships.

The Career Academies in this evaluation had the strongest and most pervasive effect on the engagement of high-risk students. For these students, the Academies reduced dropout rates and increased attendance and credits earned in both academic and career or technical courses. For the medium- and low-risk students, the Academies were able to increase exposure to career-related courses and career development experiences without reducing the likelihood of completing at least a basic academic core curriculum.

The Academies in this evaluation appeared to have less influence on curriculum content and teachers' instructional practice than on the measures mentioned above. Academy students were more likely to take career-related courses than their non-Academy peers, but the academic and career-related courses that they took were generally typical of those offered in the regular school environment — probably because Academy teachers were bound by the same requirements regarding the scope and sequence of the curriculum in their courses as were their non-Academy counterparts.

Similarly, although the Academies were somewhat more likely to expose students to applied and work-related learning activities, they typically did not integrate academic and career-related curricula and instructional practice in ways consistent with practices that have been identified in other research.[13] Such integration requires offering more extensive development opportunities to teachers — over and above the in-service workshops normally available through school and district resources — than most of the Academies could provide. Other professional development opportunities, such as shared planning time for teachers, were focused on student-related concerns and on coordinating the career development and employer-related activities.

Given the similarity between Academy and non-Academy academic curricula and instructional practice, it is not surprising that the Academies did not affect students' standardized test scores. Still, Academy students performed at least as well as their non-Academy counterparts on standardized tests and received the added benefits of participating in a combined academic and career-related curriculum and in a series of career development activities.

Finally, the attrition rates among the students selected to enroll in the Academies were high. In all, one-third of those who initially enrolled left before their scheduled high school graduation. In addition, approximately 12 percent of the applicants who were randomly assigned to the Academy group never enrolled at all. It is unclear how much of the attrition could have

---

[13]For a review of research on approaches to integrating academic and vocational education, see Grubb (1995a, 1995b).

been influenced or avoided by the Academies. Student mobility, usually owing to family circumstances that the Academies were unlikely to be able to affect, accounted for about one-quarter of the attrition; students' own choices accounted for more than one-half. But even the latter type of attrition may not stem from shortcomings of the Academy model or its implementation: Many students who left the Academies did so because they wished to take advantage other classes, programs, or opportunities that better suited their interests and needs.

The high attrition rates do suggest, however, that there is not a high level of demand for Academies, at least under circumstances where students can choose to leave and staff can ask students to leave. In any case, these circumstances represent those under which Career Academies typically operate. As a result, Academies may be able to influence students' behavior and performance for only a year or two before students move on to other opportunities. In an effort to provide the most policy-relevant information about Academies' potential to affect students' behavior, this evaluation takes the reality of attrition squarely into account by including in the analysis all students who were randomly assigned to Academies, whether they remained enrolled or not.

Before the assessment of Career Academies' effects on high school completion and initial transitions to post-secondary education and employment is presented, the next section describes the data sources used in this analysis and highlights several important issues that help frame the interpretation of the findings.

III. Data and Analysis Issues

A. Data Sources

The primary data for this report were obtained from a survey administered to students in the study sample approximately 14 months after their scheduled graduation from high school: the Career Academies Evaluation Post-High School Survey.[14] In the survey, students were asked whether and when they had graduated from high school or received a General Educational Development (GED) certificate and whether and when they enrolled in post-secondary education programs and institutions. Students who were enrolled in post-secondary education programs were asked about the programs' characteristics and about their level of engagement in them. The Post-High School Survey also requested information about students' work experiences during the year after scheduled graduation from high school, including the jobs they held, how their employment may have been connected to career-related activities during high school, and how their work experience might be preparing them for the future. Finally, the survey asked students about other experiences in their lives and their plans for the future.

The findings in this report are based on the sample of 1,482 students who completed the Post-High School Survey. These students represent 84 percent of the 1,764 students in the full study sample: 85 percent of the Academy group and 83 percent of the non-Academy group. The

---

[14]In this report, the follow-up period is sometimes referred to simply as the "year after scheduled graduation" or the "year after high school."

overall level of these response rates — and their comparability between the research groups — are very high by the standards of survey research. In addition, there were no systematic differences in background characteristics between the Academy and non-Academy group members who responded to the Post-High School Survey. In short, the relatively high response rates and the comparability of the Academy and non-Academy group members who responded afford high confidence that the survey data will yield valid estimates of the Career Academies' impacts.[15]

The evaluation also obtained high school transcript records for 86 percent of the students who completed the Post-High School Survey. The transcript data include information about attendance and course-taking patterns through the end of the scheduled 12th-grade year or until the point of dropping out of high school. This sample of students and these data permit examination of high school engagement and performance outcomes in the context of students' subsequent transitions to post-secondary education and the labor market.[16]

The report also compares outcomes for students in the non-Academy group with those for a sample of students from the National Education Longitudinal Study (NELS) of 1988 through 1994 (here called the *NELS sample*).[17] NELS administered surveys in 1988, 1990, 1992, and 1994 to a nationally representative group of students who were 8th-graders in the spring of 1988 and were scheduled to graduate from high school in 1992. Because virtually all the students in the non-Academy group completed the 9th grade, the analyses presented here include only students from the NELS sample who were 10th-graders in 1990 (that is, who did not drop out before the 10th grade). Also, to maintain comparability with the schools in the Career Academies Evaluation, only NELS students from nonselective public comprehensive high schools in urban school districts were included in the comparisons presented here.

The report presents outcomes for three subsamples of students in the NELS database: those who reported being enrolled in an academic or college preparatory program in their high school, those who reported being enrolled in their high school's general curriculum program, and those who reported being enrolled in a career, technical, or vocational program. The findings presented in this report for the NELS sample reflect outcomes and experiences through approxi-

---

[15]For a more detailed discussion of the Post-High School Survey response rates and analysis issues related to data availability, see the Technical Resources for this report (Kemple, 2001). Further analysis revealed a difference between the response rates of those who dropped out of high school before the end of their 12th-grade year and those who remained in high school. The response rate was particularly low among dropouts from the non-Academy group relative to dropouts from the Academy group. To test the sensitivity of the impact estimates to these response patterns, in the Technical Resources for this report Kemple (2001) presents impact estimates using sampling weights intended to correct for the differential survey response rates. In brief, this analysis indicates that the use of sampling weights does not change the pattern of results presented in this report.

[16]For some sites, the transcript data also included information about whether students graduated from high school. This afforded the opportunity to cross-check students' self-reported graduation status from the Post-High School Survey with the status recorded in high school transcripts. Graduation information from both transcripts and the survey were available for 670 students. Overall, only 3 percent of the students in this sample had transcript indicators for graduation, remaining in school, or dropping out that conflicted with their self-reports. For example, of those who reported graduating on time, 91 percent also had a graduation indicator in their transcript records. For most of the remaining students, there were indicators that they had transferred between schools or were still enrolled at the end of the 12th grade (neither of these statuses was considered inconsistent with a self-report of on-time graduation).

[17]National Center for Education Statistics, 1996, 1999.

mately 14 months after students' scheduled graduation from high school (through approximately August 1993). The findings on these measures were regression-adjusted and mean-centered to reflect outcomes for students who had the same distribution of background characteristics as non-Academy students in the Career Academies Evaluation.[18]

B. Analysis Issues

This section describes four analysis issues that are critical to interpreting the impact findings: distinguishing between program outcomes and program impacts, the statistical significance of impact estimates, sources of variation in impacts, and the relationship between program participation and impacts.

Outcomes versus impacts. When examining the effectiveness of Career Academies, it is important to distinguish between measures of program outcomes and measures of program impacts. In this report, *outcomes* are measures of student engagement, performance, behaviors, achievement, and attitudes. The report examines three broad categories of outcomes:

1. high school completion status;

2. post-secondary education enrollment, completion, and continuation status; and

3. employment experiences and job characteristics.

Table 1 provides definitions of the key outcome measures presented in the report.

An *impact* is defined as the effect that a Career Academy has on an outcome. Considered alone, the average outcome levels for students in the Academy group are misleading indicators of the difference that the Academies made. Previous research and prior experience highlight the fact that there are many reasons why students succeed or fail in high school that are not related to a special intervention like a Career Academy; thus, a positive outcome for the Academy group might have nothing to do with the Academies. More importantly, Academy students are exposed to many of the same opportunities and problems within the broader high school context that may enhance or limit their success in school and beyond. In order to determine the impact, or *value added*, of a Career Academy, it is necessary to compare the experiences of a group of students who were selected to enroll in an Academy (the Academy group) with a group of students with the same characteristics who were not selected to enroll (the non-Academy group).

As discussed earlier, the Academy and non-Academy groups were created using random assignment, which is widely acknowledged as the best way to ensure that there are no systematic differences between research groups initially. The outcomes for the non-Academy group are the best indicators of how students in the Academy group would have fared if they had not had access to the programs. Therefore, the impacts — that is, the differences in outcomes between the Academy and the non-Academy groups — represent the changes that the Career Academies produced over and above what students were likely to achieve in non-Academy environments.

---

[18]For a detailed description of the analyses that form the basis of these findings, see the Technical Resources for this report (Kemple, 2001).

Table 1

Definitions of the Outcome Measures Used in the Analysis

Term	Definition
Basic academic core curriculum	At least four years of English, three years of social studies, two years of mathematics, and two years of science; or at least 13 year-long academic courses
Basic academic core curriculum plus a career/vocational focus	Basic academic core curriculum plus at least three year-long career or vocational courses
Graduated on time	Received a high school diploma by the end of June in the year of scheduled graduation
Graduated late	Received a high school diploma after June in the year of scheduled graduation
Earned a GED	Earned a GED or another high school certificate
Bachelor's degree program	Any program conferring a bachelor's degree upon completion
Associate's degree program	Any program conferring an associate's degree upon completion
Skills training program	Any program conferring a certificate or license upon completion
Completed skills training program	Earned a certificate or license during the follow-up period
Ever employed	Ever worked for pay during the follow-up period
Ever employed full time	Ever worked for at least 30 hours per week during the follow-up period
Primary job	Job at which the sample member worked the greatest number of months during the follow-up period

35

Many of the outcome measures presented in the figures and tables in this report show the percentages of students in the Academy and non-Academy groups who attained a given status or reported a given behavior or experience. For example, some figures and tables report the percentages of students who graduated from high school or received a GED, enrolled in a four-year or a two-year college, or worked at a full-time job. Each figure or table compares the percentage of Academy group students who experienced a given outcome with the percentage of non-Academy group students who did so. The difference between the groups on each outcome represents the impact of the Career Academies on that outcome.

Statistical significance. Another issue of interpretation concerns the statistical significance of impact estimates. *Statistical significance* is a measure of the degree of certainty one may have that a nonzero impact truly differs from zero. If an impact estimate is statistically significant, then one may conclude with confidence that the program really made a difference. If an impact estimate is not statistically significant, then the nonzero estimate is likely to be the product of chance. The notes to the tables and figures in this report indicate whether the impact estimates shown are statistically significant at the 10 percent level (or lower). Thus, for an impact to be statistically significant, the probability that the difference is solely a result of chance must be .10 (or lower).

Statistical significance does not directly reflect the magnitude or importance of an impact estimate — only the likelihood that an impact actually occurred. In general, statistical significance is a function of two factors: the size of the sample on which an impact estimate is based and the variation, or spread, of the impact in that sample. Smaller sample sizes and greater variation yield less reliable impact estimates (that is, estimates in which one can have less confidence) than are possible when samples are larger and variation is smaller. The full sample for this evaluation is large enough to reveal moderately sized yet policy-relevant impacts at the 10 percent (or lower) level of statistical significance. Impacts of this size and relevance would include, for example, a reduction in the dropout rate or an increase in the high school graduation rate of 5 percentage points or more. For impacts in the medium-risk subgroup (which comprises only half of the full sample) to be detectable, they would have to be larger. For even smaller subgroups, such as the high- and low-risk subgroups (each of which comprises about one-quarter of the full sample), even large impacts of great relevance to policy may not be statistically significant at the 10 percent level (or lower) because of the small sample sizes and the high degree of variation in such samples.

In short, an impact estimate of a given magnitude that is statistically significant for the full sample or for a large subgroup may not be statistically significant for a smaller subgroup. An impact that is not statistically significant should be interpreted cautiously because it may be due to chance rather than to a true effect of the Career Academies.

Variation in impacts. The discussion of findings focuses on outcome measures and impact estimates that are aggregated across all the students and all the sites in the evaluation. As noted above, each of the participating Academies had implemented the core elements of the approach — at least to a basic threshold level — and each attempted to deliver similar types of services and curricula. The aggregate results thus build on these common features and provide particularly useful insights into how the Academies affected the average student in the sample under the typical conditions under which the programs operate.

At the same time, the aggregate findings mask possible variation in the extent to which the Academies were more effective for some students than for others. To explore this possible variation in impacts, the evaluation has also disaggregated findings by subgroups of students based on their background characteristics, most notably based on characteristics associated with dropout risk. As discussed later in the report, the risk subgroups exhibit particularly dramatic differences in outcome levels. Interestingly, however — and with the exception of a few outcomes for the high-risk group — the subgroups exhibit generally similar patterns of impacts.

Analyses conducted for this report also investigated variation in impacts across the nine participating sites to explore the extent to which Academies may have been more effective under some conditions than others. Because these findings were inconclusive, they are not presented in the report. There was no pattern of statistically significant variation in most of the impact estimates across the sites.[19] Other analyses attempted to assess the variation in impacts across subsets of the sites. For example, previous reports from the evaluation highlighted several dimensions of program implementation or local context that distinguished one group of sites from the others.[20] The analyses presented in this report likewise revealed no consistent or systematic variation in impacts across these groups. In a few strands of these analyses, one or two of the sites stood out as having generally positive (or negative) impacts on some outcomes. Even in these cases, however, the patterns of impacts did not vary with distinctive features of program implementation, local context, types of students served, or patterns of enrollment and attrition. In view of the general similarity of impacts across the sites, this report focuses on aggregated findings.

Impacts and program participation. A final analysis issue concerns the relationship between the amount of time that students were enrolled in the Career Academies and the impacts that the programs had on students' success in high school and beyond. As noted above, student attrition is a naturally occurring feature of Career Academies and, in fact, of high schools in general. As discussed in previous reports from this evaluation, one-third of students in the Academy group eventually left the Academy in which they enrolled (and a small percentage of students in the non-Academy group were inadvertently allowed to enroll in an Academy). In addition, the background characteristics of students who remained enrolled in the Academies differed from those who enrolled for a time and then left, making it difficult to make an unbiased estimate of the impacts that the Academies had for students who remained in their programs.

---

[19]A general F-test was performed to check whether the impact estimates are statistically similar across the sites. The F-test indicated that this hypothesis could not be rejected, suggesting that the results could be aggregated across the sites.

[20]For example, Kemple and Snipes (2000) identified one group of sites where the Career Academies represented a particularly dramatic contrast with the non-Academy school environment in terms of the extent to which students reported receiving high levels of interpersonal support from their teachers and peers (referred to as "high-contrast" sites). In the remaining schools (referred to as "low-contrast" sites), the Academies represented less of a contrast with the non-Academy environment along this dimension. Kemple, Poglinco, and Snipes (1999) identified another configuration of the sites where one group had implemented a particularly highly structured approach to organizing the partnerships with employers and career development activities for students. The remaining sites had implemented less structured employer partnerships. General F-tests were also applied to a comparison of impacts across each of these subgroups of sites. These tests did not reveal a consistent pattern of systematic differences in impacts across the site subgroups.

For example, high-risk students in the Academy group were less likely than medium- and low-risk students to enroll in a Career Academy and were more likely to have left the programs if they did enroll. If high-risk students (including those who dropped out of high school altogether) were excluded from the Academy group but included in the non-Academy group, then comparisons between the groups would systematically overestimate the impacts of the Academy programs. In other words, if the high-risk (and less engaged) Academy students were excluded from the analysis, then it would appear that the Academies increased student engagement more than they actually had. However, there were also students who left the Academies who were highly engaged in school but wished to move on to a school environment that was better suited to their evolving needs and interests. If these students were excluded from the Academy group but included in the non-Academy group, then it would appear that the Academies reduced student engagement.

In order to produce unbiased estimates of the Academies' impacts, therefore, the primary analysis conducted for the evaluation includes all students in the Academy and non-Academy groups, regardless of their Academy enrollment status at any point after random assignment. In this way, the findings reflect the impact of Career Academies under real-world conditions, which include a high rate of student attrition. Studying Career Academies under these conditions is arguably the most policy-relevant approach.

Of course, it is highly unlikely that the Career Academies had much effect on students in the Academy group who never enrolled in the programs. Nor can it be assumed that the Academies had no effect on students in the study's non-Academy group who were allowed to enroll in the programs inadvertently. From this perspective, the impact estimates may be perceived as being diluted by the inclusion of some students in the Academy group who never enrolled in the programs and the small proportion of non-Academy group members who were inadvertently allowed to enroll. It is therefore useful to examine impact estimates that account for these "crossovers" in research status, particularly estimates that indicate the *impact per enrollee* on each outcome. The impact per enrollee can be interpreted as the impact from actually enrolling in an Academy as opposed to simply being recruited and selected for admission.[21]

Adjusting for crossovers does not substantially change the overall pattern of impacts discussed in this report. For students who completed the Post-High School Survey, 87 percent of the Academy group enrolled in an Academy for at least one semester during high school, and 7 percent of the non-Academy group did so. The impact per enrollee adjustment is obtained by dividing the observed impact estimates by the difference between these rates, .8, which is equivalent to multiplying each impact estimate by 1.25. (If the percentage of students who enrolled in an Academy had been 100 percent in the Academy group and 0 percent in the non-Academy group, then the difference between the rates would be 1.0, and no adjustment would be necessary.) As

---

[21]This adjustment, which was proposed by Bloom (1984) and Orr et al. (1996), relies on two important assumptions: (1) that selection for the Academy group had no effect on students who did not enroll in an Academy and (2) that the average outcome levels for non-Academy students who were inadvertently allowed to enroll would have been the same if they had been assigned to the Academy group initially. Thus, the adjustment can be seen as discounting both the zero impact for the Academy group members who did not enroll in the program and the nonzero impact for the non-Academy group members who got the same treatment as the Academy enrollees.

discussed in the report, most of the impact estimates are not sufficiently large to have this adjustment make them much larger or more policy-relevant.[22]

IV. Outcomes and Impacts for the Full Sample

A. The Non-Academy Group's Outcomes: A Benchmark for Measuring the Impacts of Career Academies

As noted earlier, the only difference between the non-Academy group and the Academy group at the outset of the study was that non-Academy group members were not selected to enroll in an Academy. The outcomes for the non-Academy group are therefore the best indicators of what the Academy group's outcomes would have been in the absence of the opportunity to attend an Academy. A central theme in this report is that the non-Academy group's outcomes set a formidable standard for the Academy group to surpass. Even without access to an Academy, 87 percent of the non-Academy group graduated from high school or received a GED, 55 percent enrolled in a post-secondary education degree program, and 87 percent were employed during the year after high school.

This section places these outcome levels in the context of those for a nationally representative group of similar students, namely, the three NELS subsamples described above. In brief, the non-Academy group attained graduation rates and post-secondary outcomes as high as or higher than those attained by similar students nationally, indicating that the Academies attracted students who were highly likely to graduate and pursue post-secondary education even without enrolling in the programs. Thus, the students in the Academy group had to surpass national averages in order to do better than the non-Academy group, that is, for the Academies to have had a positive impact on them.

High school completion rates. Figure 2 shows the percentage of students in the non-Academy group and the NELS sample who graduated from high school or received a GED within 14 months of their scheduled graduation. It shows that 74 percent of the non-Academy group graduated from high school on time, 7 percent graduated late, and 5 percent received a GED. In all, 86 percent of non-Academy group members received a high school diploma or a GED.

Figure 2 indicates that students in the non-Academy group were somewhat more likely to graduate on time than similar students nationally who were enrolled in career or technical programs (64 percent) or the general curriculum program (69 percent) in their high schools. The NELS students in these two types of programs were more likely than the non-Academy group members to graduate late, and, as a result, their high school graduation rates during the 14 months after scheduled graduation were similar to those of the non-Academy group. The NELS students who were

---

[22]For tables that include the impact per enrollee, which is defined as the observed impact divided by the difference between the percentages of Academy and non-Academy students who ever enrolled in an Academy, see the Technical Resources for this report (Kemple, 2001).

Figure 2

High School Completion Rates
for the Non-Academy Group and the NELS Sample

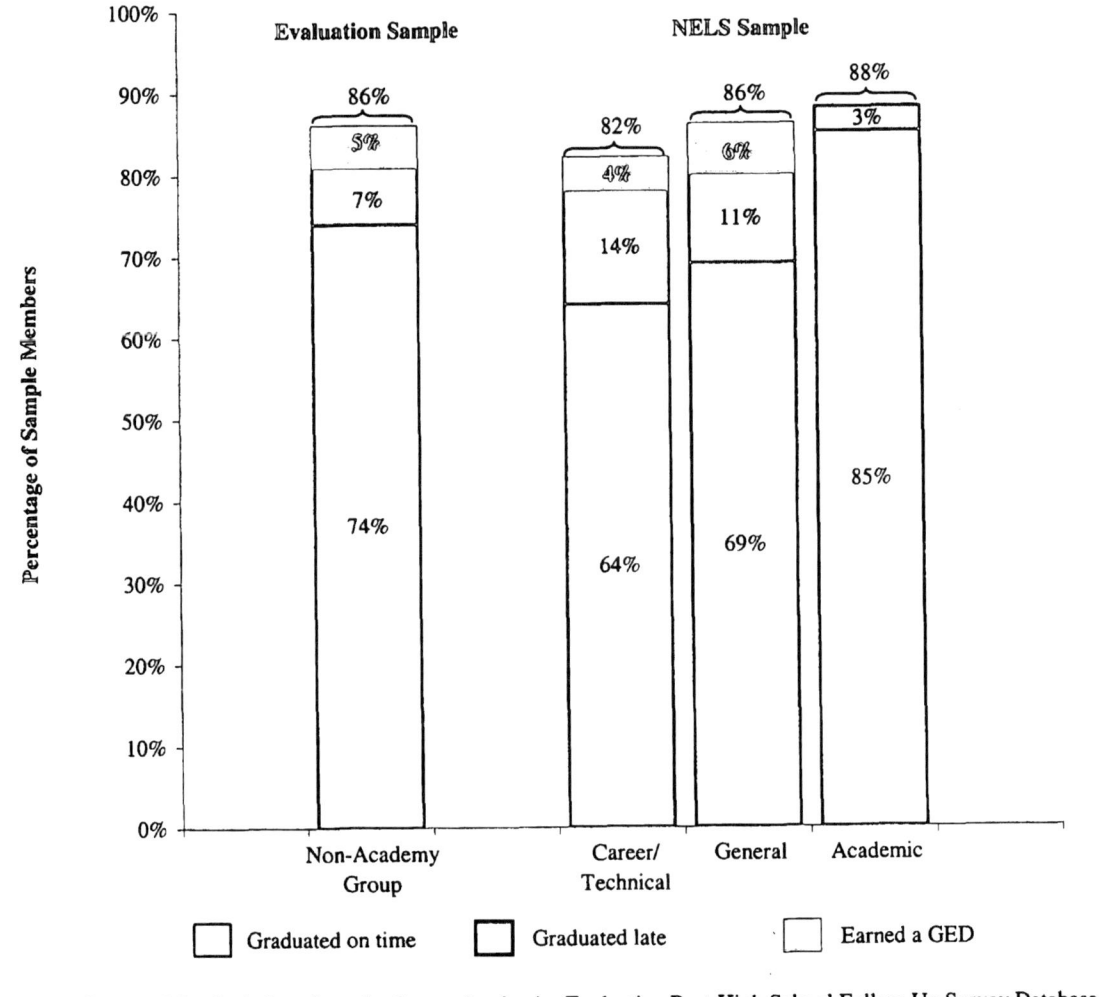

SOURCE: MDRC calculations from the Career Academies Evaluation Post-High School Follow-Up Survey Database and the National Education Longitudinal Study (NELS), 1988-1994 data.

NOTES: All measures reflect status at the end of August in the year following scheduled high school graduation.

Students were considered on-time graduates if they received their diploma by the end of June in the year they were scheduled to graduate.

The NELS sample includes only students who were enrolled in a nonselective urban public high school in 10th grade.

MDRC estimates were regression-adjusted using ordinary least squares, controlling for background characteristics.

The NELS estimates were regression-adjusted and mean-centered to reflect outcomes for students who had the same distribution of background characteristics as non-Academy sample members.

No tests of statistical significance were performed.

enrolled in academic or college preparatory programs were more likely to graduate on time and less likely to receive a GED (as opposed to a high school diploma) than were non-Academy students.

Post-secondary education enrollment. Figure 3 shows the percentages of students in the non-Academy group and the NELS sample who enrolled in some type of post-secondary education degree program — that is, a four-year bachelor's degree program, a two-year associate's degree program, or a skills training program — at some point during the 14 months after scheduled high school graduation. Of the 55 percent of the non-Academy group members who attended a post-secondary education program, about half (or 28 percent of all students in the non-Academy group) enrolled in a two-year associate's degree program.

Overall, the non-Academy students were more likely to enroll in some type of post-secondary education program than the students in the NELS sample who were in general curriculum or career or technical programs. The students in the non-Academy group were about as likely to enroll in some type of post-secondary program as the students in the NELS sample who were in the academic or college preparatory programs. The largest difference between the non-Academy group and the national sample is in the rate of enrollment in a bachelor's degree program. Whereas 26 percent of the NELS students in academic programs enrolled in a bachelor's degree program, only 16 percent of non-Academy group members did so. At the same time, 28 percent of students in the non-Academy group enrolled in an associate's degree program, compared with only 17 percent to 19 percent of the three NELS subsamples.

Employment. Figure 4 presents data on labor market participation during the 14 months after scheduled high school graduation for the non-Academy group and the NELS sample. Overall, 87 percent of non-Academy group members were employed at some point. This employment rate is comparable to that for similar students nationally who were enrolled in career or technical or general education programs in high school and somewhat higher than that for similar students nationally who enrolled in academic or college preparatory programs.

As discussed in previous reports, this evaluation sought to include schools with relatively high dropout rates and Academies that made specific attempts to serve students who were perceived to be at risk of dropping out of high school (as well as those who were doing well in school). Thus, one might expect students in the non-Academy group to have had considerably lower high school graduation and post-secondary education enrollment rates than the nationally representative NELS sample. In fact, the rates for the non-Academy group were about the same or, in some cases, higher than those for the national subsamples (the rates were particularly high relative to those for the NELS students enrolled in career or technical programs). These findings indicate that, though there is room for improvement, the Academies attracted applicants who — even without being selected to enroll in the Academies — were highly likely to graduate from high school and pursue post-secondary education.

B. Impacts for the Full Study Sample

With this context in mind, the Career Academies' impacts on high school graduation, post-secondary education enrollment, and employment outcomes are now directly assessed by comparing the outcomes for the Academy group with those for the non-Academy group. The

Figure 3
Post-Secondary Enrollment Rates
for the Non-Academy Group and the NELS Sample

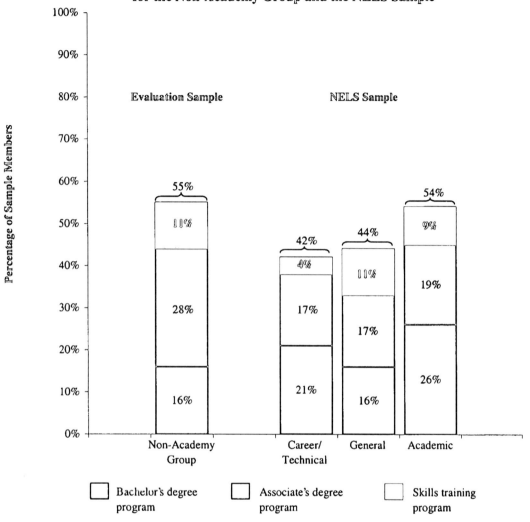

SOURCE: MDRC calculations from the Career Academies Evaluation Post-High School Follow-Up Survey Database and the National Education Longitudinal Study (NELS), 1988-1994 data.

NOTES: All measures reflect the highest degree program in which students had enrolled by the end of August in the year following scheduled graduation. Students must have earned a high school diploma or GED to be considered enrolled in these programs.

The NELS sample includes only students who were enrolled in a nonselective urban public high school in 10th grade.

MDRC estimates were regression-adjusted using ordinary least squares, controlling for background characteristics.

The NELS estimates were regression-adjusted and mean-centered to reflect outcomes for students who had the same distribution of background characteristics as non-Academy sample members.

No tests of statistical significance were performed.

-22-

42

Figure 4
Employment Rates
for the Non-Academy Group and the NELS Sample

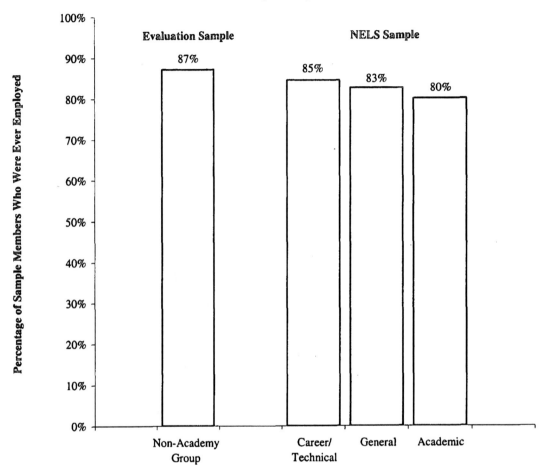

SOURCE: MDRC calculations from the Career Academies Evaluation Post-High School Follow-Up Survey Database and the National Education Longitudinal Study (NELS), 1988-1994 data.

NOTES: Ever employed means having worked for pay during the 14-month follow-up period.

The NELS sample includes only students who were enrolled in a nonselective urban public high school in 10th grade.

MDRC estimates were regression-adjusted using ordinary least squares, controlling for background characteristics.

The NELS estimates were regression-adjusted and mean-centered to reflect outcomes for students who had the same distribution of background characteristics as non-Academy sample members.

No tests of statistical significance were performed.

general finding is that, on average, students in the Academy group attained virtually the same high rates of high school graduation, post-secondary education enrollment, and employment as those in the non-Academy group. In other words, the Career Academies had little or no effect on most indicators of educational attainment and labor market participation during the year after high school.[23]

Impacts on high school graduation status. Figure 5 shows that students in the Academy and non-Academy groups were equally likely to graduate from high school on time and that students in the Academy group were slightly more likely than non-Academy students to receive a GED as opposed to graduating late. Overall, however, the Academy and non-Academy groups were equally likely to graduate from high school or receive a GED during the year after scheduled graduation.

Impacts on post-secondary education enrollment rates. As Figure 6 indicates, 55 percent of both the Academy group and the non-Academy group (more than 60 percent of those in each group who graduated or received a GED) enrolled in some type of post-secondary degree program during the year after scheduled graduation. Approximately half of those who enrolled in post-secondary education (27 percent of the Academy group and 28 percent of the non-Academy group) enrolled in a two-year associate's degree program, and slightly more than a quarter enrolled in a bachelor's degree program. The remaining sample members who went on to post-secondary education enrolled in a skills training program in pursuit of a license or certificate.

Impacts on employment. Table 2 presents several indicators of labor market participation during the year after scheduled high school graduation. As the top panel of the table shows, approximately 89 percent of Academy group members and 87 percent of non-Academy group members were employed at some point. In addition, about two-thirds of both groups held a full-time job. Both the Academy and non-Academy groups worked for an average of somewhat more than 9 months during this period.

The bottom panel in Table 2, which lists three key characteristics of the primary jobs held by employed Academy and non-Academy group members, indicates that students in the two research groups who worked held jobs with similar characteristics.[24] In both groups, the average hourly wage was in the $7.15 to $7.50 range — about 40 percent higher than the federal minimum wage ($5.15 per hour) — and the average number of hours worked per week was 32 to 33.

Impacts on combining school and work. Figure 7 further examines the extent to which sample members were engaged in productive activities during the period covered by this report. The figure displays the average number of months that students spent working or attending school during the 10-month school year (September through June) after scheduled high school

---

[23]For a more detailed list of outcomes for the full sample impacts, see the Technical Resources for this report (Kemple, 2001).

[24]In Table 2, the numbers in italics include only employed members of the Academy and non-Academy groups and do not reflect the impact that Career Academies may have had on different students' capacity to find and hold jobs. This is because the background characteristics of employed Academy and non-Academy group members were not necessarily the same at the outset of the study and thus might account for any difference in sample members' finding higher- versus lower-quality jobs.

Figure 5
Impacts on High School Completion Status
for the Full Study Sample

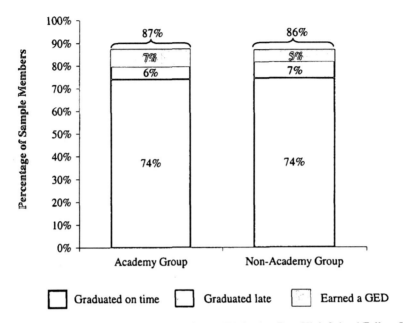

SOURCE: MDRC calculations from the Career Academies Evaluation Post-High School Follow-Up Survey Database.

NOTES: All measures reflect status at the end of August in the year following scheduled high school graduation.

Students were considered on-time graduates if they received their diploma by the end of June in the year they were scheduled to graduate.

Estimates were regression-adjusted using ordinary least squares, controlling for background characteristics.

A two-tailed t-test was applied to differences between the Academy and non-Academy groups. The difference in GED receipt was statistically signficant at the 5 percent level. No other differences between the Academy and non-Academy groups in this figure were statistically significant.

Career Academies Evaluation

Figure 6
Impacts on Post-Secondary Education Enrollment
for the Full Study Sample

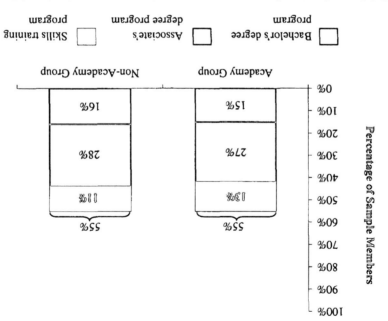

Percentage of Sample Members

Academy Group	Non-Academy Group
13%	11%
27%	28%
15%	16%
55%	55%

☐ Bachelor's degree program   ☐ Associate's degree program   ☐ Skills training program

SOURCE: MDRC calculations from the Career Academies Evaluation Post-High School Follow-Up Survey Database.

NOTES: All measures reflect the highest degree programs in which students had enrolled by the end of August in the year following scheduled graduation. Students must have earned a high school diploma or GED to be considered enrolled in these programs.

Estimates were regression-adjusted using ordinary least squares, controlling for background characteristics.

A two-tailed t-test was applied to differences between the Academy and non-Academy groups. No differences in this figure were statistically significant.

Table 2

Employment Rates and Job Characteristics
for the Full Study Sample

Outcome	Academy Group	Non-Academy Group	Impact (Difference)	Percentage Change
Employment status				
Ever employed (%)	88.7	87.2	1.5	1.7
Ever employed full time (%)	66.9	67.2	-0.3	-0.4
Held two or more jobs (%)	42.7	42.8	-0.1	-0.3
Number of months employed	9.4	9.3	0.2	2.0
Characteristics of primary job				
Average hours worked per week	*32.8*	*32.4*	*0.4*	*1.4*
Average hourly wage ($)	*7.44*	*7.17*	*0.26*	*3.7*
Average earnings per week ($)	*241.38*	*233.25*	*8.14*	*3.5*
Sample size (N=1,482)	817	665		

SOURCE: MDRC calculations from the Career Academies Evaluation Post-High School Follow-Up Survey Database.

NOTES: All measures refer to the 14-month follow-up period.

The primary job is defined as the job at which the sample member worked the greatest number of months during the 14-month follow-up period.

Percentage change equals the impact divided by the non-Academy group average.

Estimates were regression-adjusted using ordinary least squares, controlling for background characteristics.

Rounding may cause slight discrepancies in calculating differences.

Numbers in italics refer only to employed sample members. Because these numbers do not represent experimental comparisons, no tests of statistical significance were performed.

A two-tailed t-test was applied to the unitalicized differences between the Academy and non-Academy groups. No differences in this table were statistically significant.

Figure 7

Impacts on the Average Number of Months Spent Attending School or Working, for the Full Study Sample

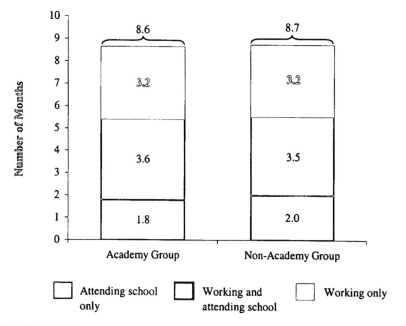

SOURCE: MDRC calculations from the Career Academies Evaluation Post-High School Follow-Up Survey Database.

NOTES: All measures reflect the average number of months spent in each status during the 10-month school year following scheduled graduation from high school.

Estimates were regression-adjusted using ordinary least squares, controlling for background characteristics.

A two-tailed t-test was applied to differences between the Academy and non-Academy groups. No differences in this figure were statistically significant.

48

graduation. Students in both the Academy and non-Academy groups spent an average of more than 8.5 months (more than 85 percent of the 10-month school year) attending school, working, or combining school and work. In all, more than 95 percent of students in the study sample spent at least 1 month during this period either working or attending school (not shown in the figure).

Figure 7 also shows that the most prevalent activity for those in both groups was combining school and work (about 3.5 months on average). The second most prevalent activity was working without attending school. Overall, sample members spent more than two-thirds of the school year working and about 55 percent of the school year attending school. Although not reflected in the figure, further analysis indicates that more than half of those in both the Academy and non-Academy groups spent at least 1 month attending school and working, and 39 percent of Academy group members and 36 percent of non-Academy group members were engaged in this combination of activities for at least 5 months.

In sum, very few of the sample members neither worked nor attended school for an appreciable period of time during the school year after scheduled high school graduation.[25] Further analyses indicate, however, that many sample members made several transitions between working, going to school, and combining the two activities. For example, only about 27 percent of those in both the Academy group and the non-Academy group spent the entire school year in the same job, education program, or combination of job and education program (not shown). In other words, nearly three-quarters of the sample members made at least one transition from school to work, from one job or education program to another, from working to not working, or the like. In fact, about 45 percent made two or more such transitions, and nearly 20 percent made three or more.[26]

The prevalence of sample members' making multiple transitions between education and employment opportunities highlights the fact that it will take several more years for many sample members to settle into patterns of activity that could pave the way to steady jobs or careers. Based on the data now available, it is difficult to predict the longer-term educational attainment and career paths of these young people.

V.   Impacts for the Risk Subgroups

Previous reports from this evaluation have highlighted the dramatic differences in outcomes among subgroups of non-Academy students in the study sample. This variation in outcome levels is also reflected in the high school graduation and post-secondary education enrollment rates. Most notably, as discussed in this section, non-Academy students in the low-risk subgroup were almost twice as likely to graduate from high school on time as those in the high-risk subgroup. They were also twice as likely to enroll in a post-secondary degree program during the year after scheduled graduation.

---

[25]Among those who did not work or attend school (about 4 percent of both the Academy group and the non-Academy group), about half were young women who were taking care of their children.

[26]It should be noted that there were no systematic differences between the Academy and non-Academy groups on these transition indicators.

Given this marked variation in outcome levels among students in the non-Academy group, an important goal of the Career Academies Evaluation has been to assess the extent to which the Academy programs may have made a larger difference for some groups of students than for others. For example, it would be difficult for the Academies to improve on the very high graduation rates of the non-Academy students in the low-risk subgroup. An important question about this group, however, is whether the Academies expanded (or at least did not limit) access to post-secondary education and the labor market. Students who began high school at relatively high risk of dropping out, in contrast, might have benefited from enrollment in an Academy in a variety of ways; for instance, the Academies could have increased their likelihood of graduating on time and of pursuing post-secondary education opportunities that might not otherwise have been available to them. This section provides an overview of the key findings for the three risk subgroups described earlier.[27]

With the exception of a few key outcomes for the high-risk subgroup, the Academies had little or no effect for all three risk subgroups. Among those in the high-risk subgroup, the Academies produced a modest (though not statistically significant) increase in the on-time graduation rate, and Academy graduates were more likely than non-Academy graduates to complete a basic academic core curriculum. For these students, the Academies also increased the likelihood of earning a license or certificate in a one-year post-secondary skills training program. Even in the high-risk subgroup, however, non-Academy students eventually graduated from high school and enrolled in a bachelor's or associate's degree program at about the same rates as Academy students. In the other subgroups, the high school completion rates, post-secondary enrollment rates, and employment rates were virtually the same for the Academy and non-Academy groups.

A. Impacts on High School Completion Status, by Risk Subgroup

Figure 8 shows the high school completion status of Academy and non-Academy students in the high-, medium-, and low-risk subgroups. The first point to notice is the dramatic differences in the on-time graduation rates across the risk subgroups. For example, whereas only 50 percent of the high-risk students in the non-Academy group graduated from high school on time, 91 percent of the low-risk students in the non-Academy group did so. Also, non-Academy students in the high-risk subgroup were much more likely to earn a GED than were non-Academy students in the low-risk subgroup. With the exception of the high-risk subgroup, however, the high school completion rates were nearly the same for the Academy and non-Academy groups.

High-risk subgroup. As Figure 8 indicates, 56 percent of the high-risk Academy students graduated from high school on time, compared with 50 percent of the high-risk non-Academy students. Although this difference is not statistically significant, it represents a 12 percent increase in the on-time graduation rate — which, if real, would be a policy-relevant effect.

---

[27]For tables showing a more detailed list of outcomes for the risk subgroups, see the Technical Resources for this report (Kemple, 2001). The Technical Resources also include tables summarizing impacts for subgroups defined by race/ethnicity, gender, and students' expectations for educational attainment measured in their 8th- or 9th-grade year.

Figure 8
Impacts on High School Completion Status,
by Risk Subgroup

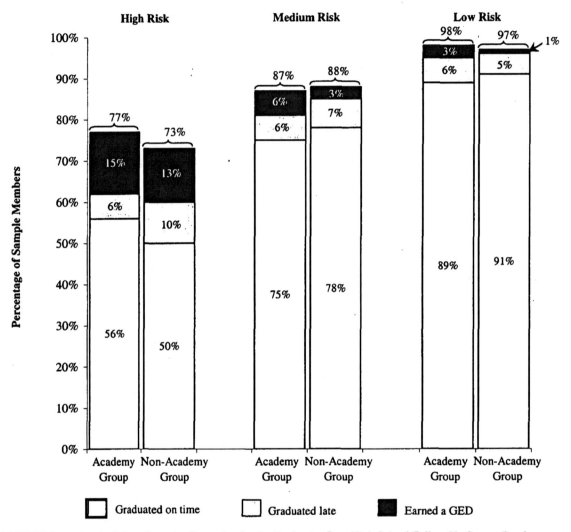

SOURCE: MDRC calculations from the Career Academies Evaluation Post-High School Follow-Up Survey Database.

NOTES: All measures reflect status at the end of August in the year following scheduled high school graduation.

Students were considered on-time graduates if they received their diploma by the end of June in the year they were scheduled to graduate.

Estimates were regression-adjusted using ordinary least squares, controlling for background characteristics.

A two-tailed t-test was applied to differences between the Academy and non-Academy groups. The difference in GED receipt in the medium-risk subgroup was statistically significant at the 5 percent level. The difference in high school graduation rates (which reflect on-time and late graduation combined) in the medium-risk subgroup was statistically significant at the 10 percent level. No other differences between the Academy and non-Academy groups in this figure were statistically significant.

Further analysis reveals some promising trends in the type of curriculum completed by on-time graduates from the high-risk subgroup. Table 3 presents the percentages of on-time graduates in the Academy and non-Academy groups who completed two types of course sequences during high school: a basic academic core curriculum and a basic academic core curriculum plus three or more career or technical courses.[28] Both of these course sequences are realizations of the dual goal of the Career Academy approach: to orient graduates toward both postsecondary education and careers.

The top panel in Table 3 shows that, among on-time graduates in the high-risk subgroup, 64 percent of the Academy group completed at least a basic academic core curriculum by the end of their 12th-grade year, and about 53 percent completed a basic academic core curriculum plus three or more career or vocational courses. In contrast, only about 49 percent of those in the non-Academy group completed at least a basic academic curriculum, and only 21 percent completed the basic academic curriculum plus three or more career or vocational courses. Thus, although the Career Academies produced only a modest (and not statistically significant) increase in the likelihood that students in the high-risk subgroup graduated from high school on time, they seem to have improved the quality of that credential in terms of the type of course sequences that on-time graduates completed.

These new findings are consistent with earlier results indicating that the Career Academies reduced high school dropout rates and increased academic course-taking among students in the high-risk subgroup. It should be noted, however, that the magnitude of the impact on the on-time graduation rate is somewhat smaller than the dropout reduction found in an earlier report. Further analysis shows that this discrepancy arises from differences between the sample of students who completed the Post-High School Survey and the sample used in the previous report.[29] Nevertheless, the reduction in the dropout rate through the end of the 12th-grade year for high-risk students appears to have translated into a comparable increase in the on-time graduation rate for this subgroup.

---

[28]The findings on course-taking patterns are derived from the evaluation's course detail records, which include high school transcript records through the end of the 12th-grade year. Thus, the estimates presented in the table do not include Academy and non-Academy group members who graduated late or received a GED. Because the background characteristics and previous school experiences of the Academy and non-Academy group members who graduated on time were not necessarily the same, any differences in these characteristics could account for differences in sample members' completing an academic curriculum. As a result, the comparisons presented in Table 3 do not reflect the impact that the Career Academies may have had on the rates of completion of these course sequences.

[29]The findings presented in Kemple and Snipes (2000) indicate that the Academies reduced the dropout rate in the high-risk subgroup by 11 percentage points. This difference is somewhat larger than the 6 percentage point increase in the on-time graduation rate reported here. The discrepancy between the two is largely due to the fact that the estimates are based on somewhat different samples of students. The findings presented in Kemple and Snipes (2000) relied primarily on the 1,454 students for whom individual school transcripts were available from the participating school districts (referred to as the School Records sample). The current report relies on the 1,482 students who completed the Post-High School Survey. Of these, 1,271 (86 percent) were also in the School Records sample. Analyses conducted for the current report indicate that the Academies reduced dropout rates and increased on-time graduation rates for high-risk students in this portion of the School Records sample by a statistically significant amount. For further information about the differences and similarities between the impact estimates derived from the two samples, see the Technical Resources for this report (Kemple, 2001).

Career Academies Evaluation

Table 3

High School Course-Taking Patterns
Among On-Time High School Graduates,
by Risk Subgroup

Outcome (%)	Academy Group Graduates	Non-Academy Group Graduates	Difference
High-risk subgroup			
Completed basic academic core	*63.8*	*48.2*	*15.5*
Completed basic academic core plus career/vocational focus	*52.5*	*21.4*	*31.1*
Sample size (n=136)	80	56	
Medium-risk subgroup			
Completed basic academic core	*79.2*	*81.0*	*-1.9*
Completed basic academic core plus career/vocational focus	*55.8*	*37.9*	*17.9*
Sample size (n=451)	240	211	
Low-risk subgroup			
Completed basic academic core	*84.1*	*88.0*	*-3.9*
Completed basic academic core plus career/vocational focus	*60.3*	*33.6*	*26.7*
Sample size (n=276)	151	125	

SOURCE: MDRC calculations from the Career Academies Evaluation Post-High School Follow-Up Survey Database and Course Detail Records Database.

NOTES: The percentages shown include only sample members who graduated on time. Complete high school transcript data were not available for those who did not graduate on time.

A basic academic core curriculum was defined as at least four years of English, three years of social studies, two years of mathematics, and two years of science; or at least 13 year-long academic courses.

A basic academic core curriculum plus a career/vocational focus was defined as the basic academic core curriculum defined above plus at least three year-long career or vocational courses.

Rounding may cause slight discrepancies in calculating differences.

Estimates were not regression-adjusted.

The numbers in italics refer only to on-time graduates. Because these numbers are not based on experimental comparisons, no tests of statistical significance were performed.

Over the course of the year after scheduled graduation, however, high-risk students in the non-Academy group essentially "caught up" with those in the Academy group. Whereas 10 percent of non-Academy students remained in school and graduated late — or, if they had dropped out, returned to school and graduated late — 6 percent of their Academy counterparts did so. This result can be seen in Figure 8. Thus, by the end of the follow-up period, 62 percent of the Academy group and 60 percent of the non-Academy group had graduated from high school.

Finally, Figure 8 indicates that a relatively high percentage of those in high-risk subgroup earned a GED. In all, approximately 15 percent of the Academy group and 13 percent of the non-Academy group earned a GED within 14 months of scheduled graduation. This is more than twice the rate among students in the NELS sample discussed earlier (see Figure 2).

Medium-risk subgroup. Figure 8 shows that, in the medium-risk subgroup, Academy students were somewhat less likely to graduate from high school than were non-Academy students. Here 81 percent of those in the Academy group graduated (on time or late), compared with 85 percent of those in the non-Academy group (a statistically significant difference). Given the difference in the GED receipt rates (also a statistically significant difference), it appears that the Academies induced some students in the medium-risk subgroup to substitute a GED for a high school diploma.

There has been considerable debate about whether a GED is equivalent to a high school diploma in terms of value in the labor market and as a credential needed to pursue further education.[30] As discussed below, however, the moderate rate of substitution of a GED for a high school diploma in the medium-risk subgroup did not affect this group's post-secondary education or labor participation patterns during the year after scheduled graduation.

Table 3 shows that, among medium-risk students who graduated on time, roughly equal percentages of Academy and non-Academy group members completed a basic academic core curriculum. The table also indicates that Academy students were much more likely than non-Academy students to have completed the basic academic core curriculum plus three or more career or technical courses. Further, completing this mixed curriculum did not reduce the medium-risk students' likelihood of completing academic courses over and above the basic core curriculum (such as foreign-language courses): Academy and non-Academy students were equally likely to earn credits in these courses (not shown).

Low-risk subgroup. As Figure 8 indicates, the Career Academies had little or no effect on the high school completion rate for the low-risk subgroup. This is not surprising given that approximately 89 percent of students in the Academy group and 91 percent of those in the non-Academy group graduated on time and that an additional 6 percent and 5 percent in the two groups, respectively, graduated late. As in the high- and medium-risk subgroups, low-risk on-time graduates in the Academy group were much more likely than those in the non-Academy group to complete a basic academic core curriculum plus three or more career or technical courses (see Table 3).

---

[30]See Cameron and Heckman, 1991; Murnane and Levy, 1996.

B. Impacts on Post-Secondary Education Enrollment, by Risk Subgroup

Figure 9 displays the rates at which Academy and non-Academy students in the high-, medium-, and low-risk subgroups enrolled in post-secondary education programs during the year after scheduled graduation.

As in Figure 8, the first point to notice in Figure 9 is the dramatic differences between the risk subgroups. Twice as many of the non-Academy students in the low-risk subgroup (72 percent) as in the high-risk subgroup (37 percent) enrolled in a post-secondary education program. In each subgroup, more than half of those who graduated from high school or earned a GED attended a post-secondary education program. Further, the majority of those who enrolled in a post-secondary education program enrolled in an associate's or a bachelor's degree program. The overall post-secondary enrollment rates for the risk subgroups are higher than those for similar students nationally, although the enrollment patterns differed somewhat across the post-secondary programs.[31]

Overall, Figure 9 indicates that there were no systematic differences in the post-secondary education enrollment rate between the Academy and non-Academy groups for any of the risk subgroups. The only exception is the rate at which student in the high-risk subgroup enrolled in and completed skills training programs (not shown).

High-risk subgroup. Figure 9 shows that 41 percent of the Academy group and 37 percent of the non-Academy group attended some type of post-secondary education program during the 14 months after scheduled high school graduation. For both groups, this percentage represents somewhat more than half of those who earned a high school diploma or GED. Academy group members were slightly more likely to enroll in a skills training program than were non-Academy group members (though this difference was not statistically significant).

Importantly, further analysis shows that the Academies substantially increased the rates at which high-risk Academy group members actually completed a skills training program and earned a license or certificate by the end of the year after scheduled high school graduation (not shown).[32] Whereas 10 percent of the Academy group earned a skills training license or certificate, only 3 percent of the non-Academy group did so (a statistically significant difference).

Further analysis also shows that there were no differences between the Academy and non-Academy groups in post-secondary education attrition. Attrition was defined as the percentage of sample members who left their post-secondary education program before completion and who did not intend to return the following year. Overall, approximately 11 percent of Academy group members left their post-secondary education program before completion, compared with 7 percent of non-Academy group members (the difference is not statistically significant).

Medium-risk subgroup. As Figure 9 illustrates, about 55 percent of medium-risk students in both the Academy and non-Academy groups enrolled in a post-secondary education degree program after high school. About 80 percent of these sample members enrolled in an

---

[31]See the Technical Resources for this report (Kemple, 2001).
[32]See the Technical Resources for this report (Kemple, 2001).

Career Academies Evaluation

Figure 9
Impacts on Post-Secondary Education Enrollment, by Risk Subgroup

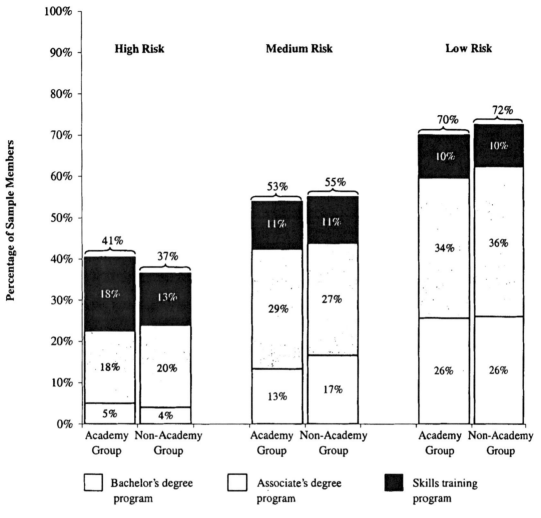

SOURCE: MDRC calculations from the Career Academies Evaluation Post-High School Follow-Up Survey Database.

NOTES: All measures reflect the highest degree programs in which students had enrolled by the end of August in the year following scheduled graduation. Students must have earned a high school diploma or GED to be considered enrolled in these programs.

Estimates were regression-adjusted using ordinary least squares, controlling for background characteristics.

A two-tailed t-test was applied to differences between the Academy and non-Academy groups. No differences in this figure were statistically significant.

associate's or a bachelor's degree program. Despite the fact that Academy group members were somewhat more likely than non-Academy group members to receive a GED rather than a high school diploma, there was no difference between the Academy and non-Academy groups on these outcomes. In other words, the slightly higher rate at which Academy group members substituted a GED for a high school diploma did not keep them from attending a post-secondary degree program.

Low-risk subgroup. Figure 9 also shows that the Academies had little or no impact on the post-secondary education enrollment rate among students in the low-risk subgroup, largely because these students were likely to attend such programs regardless of whether they had access to an Academy. Further, more than 85 percent of low-risk students who enrolled in a post-secondary program entered an associate's or a bachelor's degree program. These findings may be seen as encouraging in that, on average, the Academies did not deter highly engaged students from attending post-secondary education programs. Along with school-to-work programs, Career Academies have been criticized for not providing students, particularly those most likely to be college-bound, with the preparation needed to go on to college.

Further analysis also indicates that more than half of the Academy and non-Academy students in the low-risk group (approximately 80 percent of the low-risk students who enrolled initially) were still enrolled in a degree program at the end of the follow-up period (not shown).

C. Impacts on Employment and Job Characteristics, by Risk Subgroup

Table 4 lists the employment rates of the Academy and non-Academy groups as well as selected characteristics of the jobs held by those who were employed. Unlike the high school completion and post-secondary enrollment rates, the employment rates and job characteristics were similar across the three risk subgroups. In general, work effort — as reflected in employment rates, the number of months employed, and average hours worked per week among students who were employed — appears to have been high in all the subgroups. Students in the high-risk subgroup were somewhat more likely to be employed full time (more than 30 hours per week) than those in the medium- and low-risk subgroups, probably because students in the medium- and low-risk subgroups were more likely to be enrolled in post-secondary education programs. Finally, the average hourly wage earned by students in each of the three risk subgroups was between $7.00 and $7.50, well above the federal minimum wage of $5.15 per hour. With the exception of the average hourly wage for the medium-risk subgroup, the Academies had little or no impact on employment rates or job characteristics.

In the medium-risk subgroup, employed Academy group members held jobs that paid approximately $.55 more per hour than the jobs held by employed non-Academy group members. This finding suggests that, although Academy and non-Academy group members were equally likely to be employed, the Academy group students were able to obtain higher-wage jobs than their non-Academy group counterparts. It is also important to note that, although Academy group students obtained jobs with higher hourly wages, they were also able to pursue post-secondary education at the same rate as those in the non-Academy group.

Table 4

Employment Rates and Job Characteristics,
by Risk Subgroup

Outcome	Academy Group	Non-Academy Group	Impact (Difference)	Percentage Change
High-risk subgroup				
Employment status				
Ever employed (%)	87.6	87.7	-0.1	-0.16
Ever employed full time (%)	72.8	72.9	-0.2	-0.24
Held two or more jobs (%)	47.1	40.3	6.8	16.97
Number of months employed	9.1	9.0	0.1	0.75
Characteristics of primary job				
Average hours worked per week	*34.5*	*33.3*	*1.2*	3.59
Average hourly wage ($)	*7.38*	*7.34*	*0.04*	0.56
Average earnings per week ($)	*255.18*	*240.58*	*14.60*	6.07
Sample size (n=372)	208	164		
Medium-risk subgroup				
Employment status				
Ever employed (%)	88.9	86.8	2.1	2.37
Ever employed full time (%)	66.8	64.9	1.9	2.94
Held two or more jobs (%)	39.5	41.8	-2.3	-5.52
Number of months employed	9.6	9.4	0.3	2.85
Characteristics of primary job				
Average hours worked per week	*33.0*	*32.6*	*0.4*	1.12
Average hourly wage ($)	*7.51*	*6.95*	*0.55*	7.93
Average earnings per week ($)	*243.93*	*226.23*	*17.70*	7.83
Sample size (n=730)	396	334		
Low-risk subgroup				
Employment status				
Ever employed (%)	89.5	87.6	1.9	2.19
Ever employed full time (%)	62.1	65.1	-3.1	-4.7
Held two or more jobs (%)	45.0	46.2	-1.2	-2.61
Number of months employed	9.5	9.2	0.3	3.15
Characteristics of primary job				
Average hours worked per week	*31.1*	*30.5*	*0.6*	1.87
Average hourly wage ($)	*7.32*	*7.50*	*-0.18*	-2.4
Average earnings per week ($)	*225.23*	*237.68*	*-12.45*	-5.24
Sample size (n=380)	213	167		

(continued)

SOURCE: MDRC calculations from the Career Academies Evaluation Post-High School Follow-Up Survey Database.

NOTES: All measures refer to the 14-month follow-up period.

       Primary job is defined as the job at which the sample member worked the greatest number of months during the 14-month follow-up period.

       Percentage change equals the impact divided by the non-Academy group average.

       Estimates were regression-adjusted using ordinary least squares, controlling for background characteristics of sample members.

       Rounding may cause slight discrepancies in calculating differences.

       The numbers in italics refer only to employed sample members. Because these numbers are not based on experimental comparisons, no tests of statistical significance were performed.

       A two-tailed t-test was applied to the unitalicized differences between the Academy and non-Academy groups. No differences in this table were statistically significant.

D. Impacts on Combining School and Work, by Risk Subgroup

One criticism of school-to-work programs like Career Academies is that by promoting early entry into the labor market they may discourage students from pursuing further education. Figure 10 shows the number of months that students in the Academy and non-Academy groups spent working, attending an education program, or combining school and work during the 10-month school year after scheduled graduation. The figure indicates that the Career Academies did not promote this type of substitution and that sample members in all three subgroups spent about 7 months (or more) of the school year working, much of that time while also attending an education program.

Figure 10 indicates that Academy group members in the low-risk subgroup spent nearly half the school year both working and attending school. Low-risk students in the Academy group were slightly less likely than those in the non-Academy group to attend an education program without working (though this difference, which is not shown, is not statistically significant). In short, the Academies did not lead low-risk students to substitute work for education as some critics of school-to-work programs have suggested.

VI. Implications of the Findings

The mixed findings presented in this report have mixed implications for education policymakers and practitioners. This final section attempts to respond to some of the arguments put forth by critics and proponents of Career Academies. It also offers insights into how Academies might be enhanced to build on their strengths and address their limitations.

A. What Do the Findings Suggest About the Effectiveness of Career Academies and Related High School Reforms?

• **The findings indicate that Career Academies offer a viable pathway to high school graduation and post-secondary education.**

Career Academies have been associated most notably with career and technical education and with the school-to-work movement. Critics of Career Academies and these related education strategies have suggested that they divert students away from academic coursework during high school and limit their access to college. This critique has been offered from two perspectives. Some argue that programs like Career Academies target those who do not plan to go to college and then track them into classes and work experiences that orient them into immediate entry into the labor market. Others worry that the college-bound students who are attracted to the programs, once enrolled, are induced to substitute career or technical classes and work experience for the academic classes and experiences that would qualify them for college.

In general, the findings presented in this report suggest that — in the case of Career Academies — neither line of criticism is well founded. In all, 87 percent of the Academy group students in this study graduated from high school or completed a GED. This rate is equal to that among similar students nationally who were enrolled in general high school programs

Figure 10

Impacts on the Average Number of Months Spent Attending School or Working, by Risk Subgroup

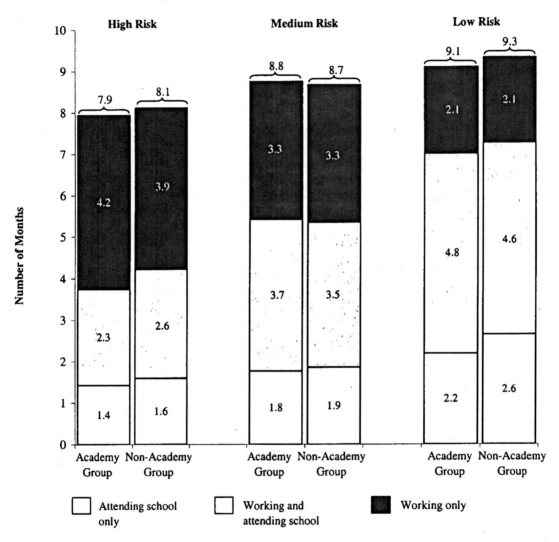

SOURCE: MDRC calculations from the Career Academies Evaluation Post-High School Follow-Up Survey Database.

NOTES: All measures reflect the average number of months spent in each status during the 10-month school year following scheduled graduation from high school.

Estimates were regression-adjusted using ordinary least squares, controlling for background characteristics.

A two-tailed t-test was applied to differences between the Academy and non-Academy groups. No differences in this figure were statistically significant.

and higher than that among similar students nationally who were enrolled in career or technical programs. On average, more than 60 percent of those who graduated from high school or re ceived a GED went on to post-secondary education. With one exception, the post-secondary enrollment rates for Academy students were as high or higher than the rates for similar students nationally, including the national sample enrolled in academic or college preparatory programs. The one exception was that Academy students were more likely to enroll in an associate's degree program as opposed to a bachelor's degree program than similar students nationally. Finally, the vast majority of Academy students were engaged in some type of productive activity (working or attending school) during most of the year after scheduled graduation from high school. Although many Academy group students worked 30 or more hours per week, this did not limit their enrollment or persistence in post-secondary education.

To the extent that the Academies in this evaluation produced impacts on educational attainment, the impacts were concentrated among those who entered the programs at the highest risk of eventually dropping out. At the same time, the Academies continued to serve a diverse population of students and did not reduce the rates at which highly engaged students graduated from high school or went on to post-secondary education.

  o   The participating Academies changed the high school environment and experiences of their students and teachers in ways that were consistent with the program's short-term goals. Yet these changes did not translate into different initial post-secondary education experiences than would have been expected for equally motivated students not enrolled in Academies.

Proponents of Career Academies and related reforms, as well as the theory of change underlying the Career Academy approach, suggest that the program represents a significant enhancement over regular high school programs for similar students. Evidence garnered from this evaluation and others indicates that Academies indeed change the high school experiences of their students in ways consistent with the goals of Academies and related education reforms.

Not surprisingly, Career Academies had the most pronounced effects on the school processes and student experiences and outcomes that are closest to the key features of the intervention. For example, the Academies' small learning communities were associated with an increase in the availability of interpersonal supports and helped high-risk students reach higher levels of school engagement, and the career focus appeared to increase the taking of career-related courses in combination with a basic academic core curriculum. In addition, the employer partnerships played a key role in increasing students' access to career development and work-related learning experiences.

Moving beyond these short-term outcomes to high school completion, post-secondary education, and labor market participation, however, the Academies' impacts appeared to dissipate. Part of the reason is that the non-Academy students — whose outcomes set the standard against which the Academy students were compared — achieved relatively high graduation rates and post-secondary education outcomes. The level of performance among the non-Academy students, who applied for the Academies but were not randomly selected to enroll in one, suggests that the Academies attracted students who were likely to graduate and move on to post-secondary education and employment regardless of whether they gained access to an Academy.

Evidence presented in a previous report from the evaluation suggests that Career Academies — though they can create conditions for maintaining and even enhancing students' engagement in high school — do not change classroom instruction substantially or affect measures of academic achievement. Similarly, many Academies do not provide supplementary college counseling services tailored for Academy students or to their needs and interests, which may explain the lack of impacts on post-secondary enrollments.

In short, it appears that the impressive education levels attained by students in this study were as likely to result from a non-Academy experience as from an Academy program. This pattern unfolded despite the substantial differences between Academy and non-Academy school environments with respect to organizational structure, career and technical course-taking patterns, and career development and school-related employment offerings that were documented in previous reports from the evaluation. It remains to be seen whether these benefits, which appeared during the high school years, will pay off for students in the longer term.

B. How Might Career Academies Build on Their Strengths and Advance Beyond Their Limitations?

It is important to recognize that the Career Academies in this evaluation provided most of their students with a pathway to graduating from high school and moving on to post-secondary education. The overwhelming majority of students from the Academy programs were working, attending school, or combining the two activities during most of the year after graduation. The comparable performance of the non-Academy group indicates that the participating high schools also provided other pathways to these post-high school outcomes. Career Academies were never intended to serve as the only route to post-secondary education.

At the same time, the results from this evaluation indicate that there is room for the Academies to improve. More than one-quarter of the Academy students in the study sample did not graduate from high school on time, and about 45 percent had not enrolled in a post-secondary education program by the end of the year after scheduled graduation. Moreover, only 15 percent of sample members enrolled in a bachelor's degree program during the year after scheduled high school graduation.

These findings challenge education policymakers and proponents of Career Academies to build on the strengths of the approach in their efforts to produce lasting impacts on high school completion and post-secondary education enrollment. Such improvements will likely be necessary if Academies are to justify the burdens they put on high schools (which, for example, have to rearrange high school schedules and organization and add to teachers' responsibilities); employer partners (who, for example, may have to involve employees in school activities, accommodate student interns, and supply extra materials and resources); and students (who, for example, may have fewer opportunities to take elective courses and may need to satisfy additional career awareness and work-based learning requirements). At this point in the evaluation, it is possible only to offer some hypotheses about how Academies may produce these improvements.

Increase high-risk students' access to Career Academies. To the extent that Academies have longer-term impacts, the impacts are concentrated among students who entered the program at high risk of dropping out. This finding suggests that Academies should make greater efforts to attract and retain such students. At the same time, targeting the programs exclusively to high-risk students might lower teachers', students', and parents' expectations of the program. More importantly, based on implementation research conducted for this evaluation, the Academies appear to draw much of their power to improve interpersonal supports and increase student engagement from the diversity of their student bodies.

Several school districts and school reform initiatives around the country are now attempting to convert entire high schools into clusters of Career Academies. Instead of giving students the option of enrolling in traditional general or vocational track programs, these wall-to-wall Academies offer students a choice among different Academies that combine academic and career-related curricula. This approach may have the greatest potential for maximizing high-risk students' access to the programs (because all students would be required to enroll in an Academy) while ensuring that the Academies include a broad mix of students. These high schools and reform initiatives, however, face the related challenges of preventing high-risk students from being tracked into poorly implemented Academies and of ensuring a high level of implementation on a larger scale.

Heighten the emphasis on meeting academic standards, and provide more intensive guidance and support for college entrance. The Academy approach has flourished partly because it offers concrete, direct responses to pressing problems facing comprehensive high schools. Judging from the findings from this evaluation, however, the approach also has limitations, notably a lack of impacts on standardized test scores and college enrollment rates. These limitations, which are common to most efforts to improve high schools, probably stem from the fact that the Career Academy approach as currently formulated does not prescribe explicit, direct strategies for raising test scores, improving instruction, or guiding students toward college. One reason why such strategies have not been central in the Academy approach is that the earliest Academies were established with narrower goals and a narrower target population than today's Academies. Moreover, setting up cohesive small learning communities, scheduling coherent blocks of academic and career course sequences, and building productive employer partnerships have proven to be significant challenges in their own right. With the recent advent of the academic standards movement and the increasingly high premium placed on post-secondary education, the Academies will need to expand beyond their original core components.

In view of the present findings, school officials and Academy administrators should consider building on the Career Academy model's existing components to prepare students to meet new academic standards and provide them with the information they need to apply for and gain admission to college. For example, school officials and Academy administrators might consider implementing an accelerated academic program in the 9th grade to help students who are behind academically catch up. In grades 10 to 12, the Academies could then focus on providing students with a rigorous academic curriculum of higher-level courses that would prepare them for high-stakes tests and help them garner the credentials needed to attend college.

A growing number of states and school districts are beginning to define more clearly the content knowledge and skills that students should learn and that teachers should teach and to develop ways to assess whether students have attained these skills. Teachers are typically provided with few opportunities to learn about the content standards for which they are held accountable or to incorporate these standards into curricula and instructional practice. Career Academies' small learning communities provide an opportunity for teachers to plan together, develop curriculum and instructional strategies aligned with the content standards, and monitor the progress of the students whom they all teach.

Most Career Academies do not have a counselor who can provide students with individualized, ongoing guidance about their post-secondary education options and the steps that they need to take to prepare for, apply to, and be admitted to college. More importantly, many students and their families — both in and outside Academies — are intimidated by the high cost of a college education and do not consider a bachelor's degree program or even an associate's degree program a realistic option. Most Academies must rely on the host high school's counselors, who are typically overwhelmed handling a wide range of guidance issues in the school. Even when they manage to concentrate on college counseling, high school counselors are typically able to focus only on students and families who take the initiative to seek out their services.

Career Academies may be able to address these limitations by building on their small learning communities, course sequences, and employer partnerships. Their school-within-a-school organization, for example, gives them the capacity to provide students with a greater degree of personalized attention, especially with regard to students' day-to-day performance and behavior in school. This student-centered environment also might be used to help students set long-term goals and prepare for post-secondary education from the beginning of their high school careers. In addition, Academies' curricula and course sequences could be designed to ensure that students will have met college entrance requirements by the time they are ready to graduate. Finally, Academies might compensate for limited college guidance capacity by calling on their employer partners to help incorporate information about strategies for pursuing post-secondary education into the Academies' career awareness and development activities and work-based learning programs.

Identify systemic problems that keep any one intervention from making a substantial difference for high school students. Several studies have documented a wide range of systemic problems that prevent students from making successful transitions from high school to post-secondary education and the labor market.[33] One strand of this research identifies the lack of active collaboration between faculty and administrators at different levels of the education system as a contributing factor. Because many colleges have established standards that high schools must follow, they do not see high schools as customers with whom they must collaborate to ensure a smooth flow of students into their institutions. High schools must also contend with multiple demands for accountability to their primary customers (students, parents, taxpayers, and so on), which may prevent them from developing clear communication with post-secondary education institutions and employers.

At the same time, several studies have documented a strong relationship between education credentials and skills development and successful transitions to stable, high-wage employment.[34] For example, the transition from school to work is easiest for college graduates and most difficult for high school dropouts. Yet the skills and credentials that students acquire in high

---

[33]See, for example, Klerman and Karoly, 1995; and Osterman and Iannozzi, 1993.
[34]See Klerman and Karoly, 1995; Murnane and Levy, 1996; and Snipes, 1998.

school and even in post-secondary education often fail to match the demands of the labor market. Further, even when young people obtain relevant credentials and skills, employers are often unable to differentiate among prospective employees except by looking at gross indicators of quality such as diplomas and degrees.

It is unrealistic to expect the Career Academy model or any other high school reform by itself to have a substantial impact on these types of systemic problems. At the same time, it is important that policymakers and practitioners who wish to promote Academies and related reforms develop a clearer understanding of the larger social, educational, and economic context in which the model will be implemented. Equipped with such understanding, they might then combine a reform such as Career Academies with initiatives aimed more explicitly at building strong links between high school and post-secondary education and the labor market. For example, the Secretary of Labor's Commission on Achieving Necessary Skills (SCANS) has been developing industry skill standards that employers will value and that education institutions can use to shape their own curricula and standards. SCANS also includes a "portable diploma" — which signifies attainment of competencies across a range of skills in a given industry or career area — that can serve as a clear indicator to prospective employers and even to education institutions of a student's suitability for a job or further education. The National Academy Foundation — a national organization sponsoring nearly 500 Career Academies in three career areas — has embarked on developing a similar credential for use by its member Academies. Other initiatives are beginning to develop new procedures and standards for boosting admissions to four-year post-secondary degree programs.[35]

C. Further Follow-Up Is Needed to Determine the Long-Term Effectiveness of Career Academies

Although the results presented in this report go beyond those presented in other research on Career Academies and in previous reports from this evaluation, the full story of Career Academies' effectiveness is still unfolding. The findings reported to date raise several issues that highlight the need to examine longer-term results before making definitive judgments about the effectiveness of the Career Academy approach.

First, earlier reports from this evaluation showed that the Academies increased students' exposure to career awareness and development activities and to work-related learning opportunities. The employer partnerships provided students with personal and structured connections to the world of work and local employers with an opportunity to help shape the workforce preparation of high school students in their communities. Academy students were also much more likely than their non-Academy counterparts to complete a sequence of career or technical courses in addition to a basic academic core curriculum. Given that most students in the study sample did not start out in career-oriented jobs, it is unlikely that such experiences would have strong effects on their transitions into the labor market during the year after high school. It will be therefore important to examine the extent to which the Academies' focus on career-related experiences during high school leads to better employment outcomes and career trajectories in the longer term.

---

[35]See Urquiola et al., 1997.

Second, previous research indicates that the year after high school graduation is a particularly unsettled period for 18- to 20-year-old youth.[36] The patterns of education and employment experiences for the students in the present sample are consistent with this evidence. For example, 40 percent of the Academy students went on to a two-year associate's degree program or a one-year training program. Many students use these types of educational opportunities as stepping-stones to four-year colleges or other programs. In addition, during the school year after scheduled graduation, about 75 percent of the sample members made at least one transition into or out of an education program, a job, or a combination of education and work; about 45 percent made two or more such transitions; and 20 percent made three or more. In view of the prevalence and likely persistence of such transitions for another year or two, it is extremely difficult to discern a career trajectory at this stage. Thus, it will be important to determine whether Academy students' more career-oriented experience helps them make smoother, more successful transitions between the options available to them.

Finally, in assessing the effectiveness of Career Academies — a school-to-career initiative — evidence about longer-term effects on educational attainment and employment outcomes should be weighed particularly heavily. Academies have a demonstrable capacity to keep students in school and to improve several key indicators of school engagement (for example, attendance and course-taking patterns) for high-risk students. Although the Academies in this study were less successful in changing curriculum and instruction and improving student achievement, the vast majority of Academy students nevertheless made successful initial transitions into post-secondary education or employment. A more definitive assessment of the strengths and limitations of the Career Academy approach should take account of evidence about their effects on longer-term outcomes.

To address these and other issues, the evaluation is collecting data on students' education and labor market experiences during the second, third, and fourth years after their scheduled high school graduation. The goal of this ongoing work is to determine whether the Academies enable students to make better choices about post-secondary education and employment and, if so, whether their choices lead to higher levels of educational attainment and entry into higher-wage, more career-oriented jobs.

---

[36]Osterman and Iannozzi, 1993.

References

Atkinson, Richard C., and Gregg B. Jackson. 1992. *Research and Education Reform: Roles for the Office of Educational Research and Improvement.* Washington, DC: National Academy Press.

Betsey, Charles L., Robinson Hollister, and Mary R. Papageorgiou (eds.). 1985. *Youth Employment and Training Programs: The Yedpa Years.* Washington, DC: Committee on Youth Employment Programs, National Research Council.

Bloom, Howard S. 1984. "Accounting for No-Shows in Experimental Evaluation Designs." *Evaluation Review* 8 (2): 225-246.

Cameron, Stephen V., and James J. Heckman. 1991. "The Nonequivalence of High School Equivalents." Cambridge, MA: National Bureau of Economic Research.

Career Academy Support Network. 2001. Web site: http://casn.berkeley.edu/.

Grubb, W. Norton (ed.). 1995a. *Education Through Occupations in American High Schools: The Challenges of Implementing Curriculum Integration,* Vol. 1. New York: Teachers College Press.

Grubb, W. Norton (ed.). 1995b. *Education Through Occupations in American High Schools: The Challenges of Implementing Curriculum Integration,* Vol. 2. New York: Teachers College Press.

Job Training Partnership Act. 1989. U.S. Public Law 97-300 (October. 13, 1982); 96 Stat. 1322; classified principally to Chapter 19, secs. 1501 et seq., of Title 29, Labor.

Kemple, James J. 1997. *Career Academies: Communities of Support for Students and Teachers — Emerging Findings from a 10-Site Evaluation.* New York: Manpower Demonstration Research Corporation.

Kemple, James J. 2001. *Career Academies: Impacts on Students' Initial Transitions to Post-Secondary Education and Employment.* Technical Resources.
Web page: http://www.mdrc.org/Reports2001/CareerAcademies/CA_TechResources.htm.

Kemple, James J., Susan M. Poglinco, and Jason C. Snipes. 1999. *Career Academies: Building Career Awareness and Work-Based Learning Activities Through Employer Partnerships.* New York: Manpower Demonstration Research Corporation.

Kemple, James, and JoAnn Leah Rock. 1996. *Career Academies: Early Implementation Lessons from a 10-Site Evaluation.* New York: Manpower Demonstration Research Corporation.

Kemple, James, and Jason C. Snipes. 2000. *Career Academies: Impacts on Students' Engagement and Performance in High School.* New York: Manpower Demonstration Research Corporation.

Klerman, Jacob Alex, and Lynn A. Karoly. 1995. "The Transition to Stable Employment: The Experience of Youth in Their Early Labor Market Career." Berkeley: University of California, National Center for Research in Vocational Education.

Maxwell, Nan, and Victor Rubin. 1997. *The Relative Impact of a Career Academy on Post-Secondary Work and Education Skills in Urban, Public High Schools.* Hayward, CA: Human Investment Research and Education Center.

Maxwell, Nan, and Victor Rubin. 1999. *Improving the Transition from School to Work: Assessing the Impact of Old and New Strategies.* Hayward, CA: Human Investment Research and Education Center.

Maxwell, Nan, and Victor Rubin. 2000. *High School Career Academies: A Pathway to Educational Reform in Urban School Districts?* Kalamazoo, MI: W. E. Upjohn Institute for Employment Research.

Murnane, Richard J., and Frank Levy. 1996. *Teaching the New Basic Skills: Principles for Educating Children to Thrive in a Changing Economy.* New York: Free Press.

National Center for Education Statistics. 1996. *National Education Longitudinal Study: 1988-94 Methodology Report.* Washington, DC: U.S. Government Printing Office.

National Center for Education Statistics. 1999. *National Education Longitudinal Study: 1988-94 Data Files and Electronic Codebook System, Base Year Through Third Follow-Up.* Washington, DC: U.S. Government Printing Office.

Orr, Larry, Howard Bloom, Stephen Bell, Fred Doolittle, Winston Lin, and George Cave. 1996. *Does Training for the Disadvantaged Work?* Washington, DC: Urban Institute Press.

Osterman, Paul, and Maria Iannozzi. 1993. "Youth Apprenticeships and School-to-Work Transitions: Current Knowledge and Legislative Strategy." Working Paper No. 14. Philadelphia: National Center on the Educational Quality of the Workforce.

Snipes, Jason C. 1998. "Skill Mismatch, Turnover, and the Development of Young Workers' Careers." Ph.D. dissertation. Cambridge, MA: Harvard University, Kennedy School of Government.

Stern, David, Charles Dayton, and Marilyn Raby. 2000. *Career Academies: Building Blocks for Reconstructing American High Schools.* Berkeley: University of California, Graduate School of Education.

Urquiola, Miguel, David Stern, Illana Horn, Carolyn Dornsife, Bernadette Chi, Lea Williams, Donna Merritt, Katherine Hughes, and Tom Bailey. 1997. *School to Work, College and Career: A Review of Policy, Practice, and Results 1993-1997.* Berkeley: University of California, National Center for Research in Vocational Education.

69

Recent Publications on MDRC Projects

Note: For works not published by MDRC, the publisher's name is shown in parentheses. With a few exceptions, this list includes reports published by MDRC since 1999. A complete publications list is available from MDRC and on its Web site (www.mdrc.org), from which copies of MDRC's publications can also be downloaded.

Education Reform

Accelerated Schools
This study examines the implementation and impacts on achievement of the Accelerated Schools model, a whole-school reform targeted at at-risk students.

Evaluating the Accelerated Schools Approach: A Look at Early Implementation and Impacts on Student Achievement in Eight Elementary Schools. 2001. Howard Bloom, Sandra Ham, Laura Melton, Julienne O'Brien.

Project GRAD
This evaluation examines Project GRAD, an education initiative targeted at urban schools and combining a number of proven or promising reforms.

Building the Foundation for Improved Student Performance: The Pre-Curricular Phase of Project GRAD Newark. 2000. Sandra Ham, Fred Doolittle, Glee Ivory Holton.

Career Academies
The largest and most comprehensive evaluation of a school-to-work initiative, this study examines a promising approach to high school restructuring and the school-to-work transition.

Career Academies: Early Implementation Lessons from a 10-Site Evaluation. 1996. James Kemple, JoAnn Leah Rock.
Career Academies: Communities of Support for Students and Teachers — Emerging Findings from a 10-Site Evaluation. 1997. James Kemple.
Career Academies: Building Career Awareness and Work-Based Learning Activities Through Employer Partnerships. 1999. James Kemple, Susan Poglinco, Jason Snipes.
Career Academies: Impacts on Students' Engagement and Performance in High School. 2000. James Kemple, Jason Snipes.

School-to-Work Project
A study of innovative programs that help students make the transition from school to work or careers.

Home-Grown Lessons: Innovative Programs Linking School and Work (Jossey-Bass Publishers). 1995. Edward Pauly, Hilary Kopp, Joshua Haimson.
Home-Grown Progress: The Evolution of Innovative School-to-Work Programs. 1997. Rachel Pedraza, Edward Pauly, Hilary Kopp.

Project Transition
A demonstration program that tested a combination of school-based strategies to facilitate students' transition from middle school to high school.

Project Transition: Testing an Intervention to Help High School Freshmen Succeed. 1999. Janet Quint, Cynthia Miller, Jennifer Pastor, Rachel Cytron.

Equity 2000
Equity 2000 is a nationwide initiative sponsored by the College Board to improve low-income students' access to college. The MDRC paper examines the implementation of Equity 2000 in Milwaukee Public Schools.

Getting to the Right Algebra: The Equity 2000 Initiative in Milwaukee Public Schools. 1999. Sandra Ham, Erica Walker.

Education for Adults and Families

LILAA Initiative
This study of the Literacy in Libraries Across America (LILAA) initiative explores the efforts of five adult literacy programs in public libraries to improve learner persistence.

So I Made Up My Mind: Introducing a Study of Adult Learner Persistence in Library Literacy Programs. 2000. John T. Comings, Sondra Cuban.
"I Did It for Myself": Studying Efforts to Increase Adult Learner Persistence in Library Literacy Programs. 2001. John Comings, Sondra Cuban, Johannes Bos, Catherine Taylor.

Toyota Families in Schools

A discussion of the factors that determine whether an impact analysis of a social program is feasible and warranted, using an evaluation of a new family literacy initiative as a case study.

An Evaluability Assessment of the Toyota Families in Schools Program. 2001. Janet Quint.

Opening Doors to Earning Credentials

An exploration of strategies for increasing low-wage workers' access to and completion of community college programs.

Opening Doors: Expanding Educational Opportunities for Low-Income Workers. 2001. Susan Golonka, Lisa Matus-Grossman.

Effects of Welfare and Antipoverty Programs on Children

Next Generation Project

A collaboration among researchers at MDRC and several other leading research institutions focused on studying the effects of welfare, antipoverty, and employment policies on children and families.

How Welfare and Work Policies Affect Children: A Synthesis of Research. 2001. Pamela Morris, Aletha Huston, Greg Duncan, Danielle Crosby, Johannes Bos.

How Welfare and Work Policies Affect Employment and Income: A Synthesis of Research. 2001. Dan Bloom, Charles Michalopoulos.

Minnesota Family Investment Program

An evaluation of Minnesota's pilot welfare reform initiative, which aims to encourage work, alleviate poverty, and reduce welfare dependence.

Reforming Welfare and Rewarding Work: Final Report on the Minnesota Family Investment Program. Volume 2: Effects on Children. 2000. Lisa Gennetian, Cynthia Miller.

Reforming Welfare and Rewarding Work: A Summary of the Final Report on the Minnesota Family Investment Program. 2000. Virginia Knox, Cynthia Miller, Lisa Gennetian.

Canada's Self-Sufficiency Project

A test of the effectiveness of a temporary earnings supplement on the employment and welfare receipt of public assistance recipients.

The Self-Sufficiency Project at 36 Months: Effects on Children of a Program That Increased Parental

Employment and Income (Social Research and Demonstration Corporation, Ottawa, Canada). 2000. Pamela Morris, Charles Michalopoulos.

National Evaluation of Welfare-to-Work Strategies

Conceived and sponsored by the U.S. Department of Health and Human Services (HHS), with support from the U.S. Department of Education (ED), this is the largest-scale evaluation ever conducted of different strategies for moving people from welfare to employment.

Do Mandatory Welfare-to-Work Programs Affect the Well-Being of Children? A Synthesis of Child Research Conducted as Part of the National Evaluation of Welfare-to-Work Strategies (HHS/ED). 2000. Gayle Hamilton.

Teen Parents on Welfare

Teenage Parent Programs: A Synthesis of the Long-Term Effects of the New Chance Demonstration, Ohio's Learning, Earning, and Parenting (LEAP) Program, and the Teenage Parent Demonstration (TPD). 1998. Robert Granger, Rachel Cytron.

Ohio's LEAP Program

An evaluation of Ohio's Learning, Earning, and Parenting (LEAP) Program, which uses financial incentives to encourage teenage parents on welfare to stay in or return to school.

LEAP: Final Report on Ohio's Welfare Initiative to Improve School Attendance Among Teenage Parents. 1997. Johannes Bos, Veronica Fellerath.

New Chance Demonstration

A test of a comprehensive program of services that seeks to improve the economic status and general well-being of a group of highly disadvantaged young women and their children.

New Chance: Final Report on a Comprehensive Program for Young Mothers in Poverty and Their Children. 1997. Janet Quint, Johannes Bos, Denise Polit.

Parenting Behavior in a Sample of Young Mothers in Poverty: Results of the New Chance Observational Study. 1998. Martha Zaslow, Carolyn Eldred, editors.

MDRC Working Papers on Research Methodology

A new series of papers that explore alternative methods of examining the implementation and impacts of programs and policies.

Building a Convincing Test of a Public Housing Employment Program Using Non-Experimental Methods: Planning for the Jobs-Plus Demonstration. 1999. Howard Bloom.

Estimating Program Impacts on Student Achievement Using "Short" Interrupted Time Series. 1999. Howard Bloom.

Using Cluster Random Assignment to Measure Program Impacts: Statistical Implications for the Evaluation of Education Programs. 1999. Howard Bloom, Johannes Bos, Suk-Won Lee.

Measuring the Impacts of Whole School Reforms: Methodological Lessons from an Evaluation of Accelerated Schools. 2001. Howard Bloom.

The Politics of Random Assignment: Implementing Studies and Impacting Policy. 2000. Judith Gueron.

Modeling the Performance of Welfare-to-Work Programs: The Effects of Program Management and Services, Economic Environment, and Client Characteristics. 2001. Howard Bloom, Carolyn Hill, James Riccio.

A Regression-Based Strategy for Defining Subgroups in a Social Experiment. 2001. James Kemple, Jason Snipes.

Extending the Reach of Randomized Social Experiments: New Directions in Evaluations of American Welfare-to-Work and Employment Initiatives. 2001. James Riccio, Howard Bloom.

72

About MDRC

The Manpower Demonstration Research Corporation (MDRC) is a nonprofit, nonpartisan social policy research organization. We are dedicated to learning what works to improve the well-being of low-income people. Through our research and the active communication of our findings, we seek to enhance the effectiveness of social policies and programs. MDRC was founded in 1974 and is located in New York City and San Francisco.

MDRC's current projects focus on welfare and economic security, education, and employment and community initiatives. Complementing our evaluations of a wide range of welfare reforms are new studies of supports for the working poor and emerging analyses of how programs affect children's development and their families' well-being. In the field of education, we are testing reforms aimed at improving the performance of public schools, especially in urban areas. Finally, our community projects are using innovative approaches to increase employment in low-income neighborhoods.

Our projects are a mix of demonstrations — field tests of promising program models — and evaluations of government and community initiatives, and we employ a wide range of methods to determine a program's effects, including large-scale studies, surveys, case studies, and ethnographies of individuals and families. We share the findings and lessons from our work — including best practices for program operators — with a broad audience within the policy and practitioner community, as well as the general public and the media.

Over the past quarter century, MDRC has worked in almost every state, all of the nation's largest cities, and Canada. We conduct our projects in partnership with state and local governments, the federal government, public school systems, community organizations, and numerous private philanthropies.

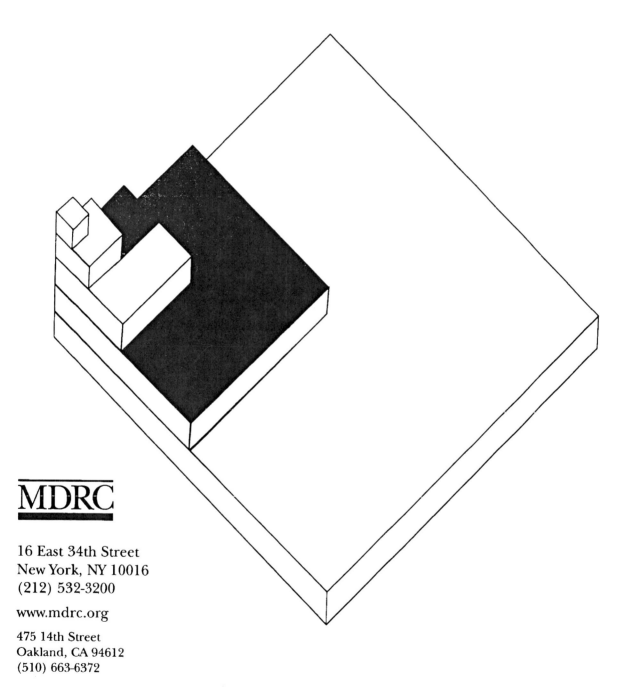

MDRC

16 East 34th Street
New York, NY 10016
(212) 532-3200

www.mdrc.org

475 14th Street
Oakland, CA 94612
(510) 663-6372

U.S. Department of Education
Office of Educational Research and Improvement (OERI)
National Library of Education (NLE)
Educational Resources Information Center (ERIC)

NOTICE

Reproduction Basis

This document is covered by a signed "Reproduction Release (Blanket)" form (on file within the ERIC system), encompassing all or classes of documents from its source organization and, therefore, does not require a "Specific Document" Release form.

This document is Federally-funded, or carries its own permission to reproduce, or is otherwise in the public domain and, therefore, may be reproduced by ERIC without a signed Reproduction Release form (either "Specific Document" or "Blanket").

EFF-089 (3/2000)

CPSIA information can be obtained at www.ICGtesting.com
Printed in the USA
BVOW03s0803070915

416887BV00007B/183/P

9 781240 626489